James Wright

Twayne's United States Authors Series

Warren French, Editor

University College of Swansea, Wales

TUSAS 494

JAMES WRIGHT
(1927–1980)
Photograph by Layle Silbert, reproduced by permission

James Wright

By David C. Dougherty

Loyola College in Maryland

Twayne Publishers
A Division of G.K. Hall & Co. • *Boston*

James Wright

David C. Dougherty

Copyright © 1987 by G.K. Hall & Co.
All Rights Reserved
Published by Twayne Publishers
A Division of G.K. Hall & Co.
70 Lincoln Street
Boston, Massachusetts 02111

Copyediting supervised by Lewis DeSimone
Book production by Janet Zietowski
Book design by Barbara Anderson

Typeset in 11 pt. Garamond
by P&M Typesetting, Inc., Waterbury, Connecticut

Printed on permanent/durable acid-free paper
and bound in the United States of America

Library of Congress Cataloging in Publication Data

Dougherty, David C.
  James Wright.

  (Twayne's United States authors series ; TUSAS 494)
  Bibliography: p. 150
  Includes index.
  1. Wright, James Arlington, 1927–1980—Criticism
and interpretation.   I. Title.   II. Series.
PS3573.R5358Z65   1987   811'.54   86-29588
ISBN 0-8057-7496-3 (alk. paper)

Contents

Foreword
About the Author
Preface
Acknowledgments
Chronology

Chapter One
The Life and Times of James Wright   1

Chapter Two
"The Beautiful Language of My Friends":
The Green Wall and *Saint Judas*   18

Chapter Three
"The Kind of Poetry I Want":
The Branch Will Not Break   49

Chapter Four
"This Scattering Poem": *Shall We Gather at the River*
and "New Poems"   69

Chapter Five
"My Ohioan": *Two Citizens*   93

Chapter Six
"The Inmost Secret of Light": The Final Volumes   113

Chapter Seven
"The Poetry of a Grown Man"   141

Notes and References   145
Selected Bibliography   150
Index   155

Foreword

Professor Dougherty has traced the progress and change in James Wright's poetry with sensitive insight. In a different capacity, that of wife and involved observer, I witnessed progress and change too.

James had almost completed *Shall We Gather at the River* when we met. I heard some of the poems from that manuscript at readings and possessed a worn and much folded copy of "The Lights in the Hallway," which he had typed out in his room at the Hotel Regent and mailed to me without comment.

The hallway he referred to was in the reconverted tenement house where I lived. In conversations about his first visit to my ground floor apartment, James always mentioned that hallway, how long the distance had seemed from the little foyer where he stood to the open doorway where I was. I remember how I watched him come down the hall toward me carrying a bouquet of roses and a brown paper bag. In the bag were copies of his three books, purchased that day for me at the Gotham Book Store.

James was in the last stages of work for *Shall We Gather at the River* when we married. I regarded with close attention the mixture of pain, relief, and anxiety he experienced when the finished manuscript was mailed to Wesleyan University Press and the time and labor devoted to the correction of proofs. In the next thirteen years I would be witness to the same procedure as James compiled *Collected Poems*, translated two works by Hermann Hesse, completed two more books of his own poetry, two chapbooks of prose pieces and prepared *This Journey*.

After *Collected Poems* was published our life became established and took on a pleasant pattern. We moved to a larger apartment across the street from the house with the lights in the hallway. James was intent on work and students at Hunter College. When his pocket was picked on the 86th Street crosstown bus he bragged that at last he had become a real New Yorker. We had time on weekends to see friends, go to old movies, walk in the park or relax at Lake Minnewaska, a lovely resort in the mountains not far from New York. In the summer we usually traveled.

There were changes in the way James worked too. He began to

spend more time with a journal and made daily entries in the little, brown notebook always kept in his pocket. He returned to the habit, once observed in graduate school, of using the early morning for work. He would get up before breakfast, sit in his favorite orange armchair by the living room windows and spend several hours in serious reflection, a cup of coffee beside him, the radio turned low to a classical music station. At 8:00 he would bring me coffee and go into his study to work at the typewriter, perhaps to transpose the poem or prose piece composed in that time of quiet thought from his journal to a large notebook. Then he was ready for the business of the day; preparation for classes, correspondence, or a trip to the laundromat, one of his home chores.

Poems about Europe were another change. *Two Citizens,* that fierce and uneven book, is filled with places and people discovered on our first trip: heads of babies and leaves of strawberry plants chiseled on the Cathedral of Chartres by long dead stonecutters, the bell at Fiesole as it swung in and out of a slender tower, the old man who greeted us every day in the Café de la Ville at St. Benôit and directed us to the grave of Max Jacob, wild flowers at Lake Ohrid and the sun of Italy.

Several years after that first trip James found Verona on the Adige River. From the moment he stepped out of the train station at Verona it became his city. We returned again and again; explored the old streets, walked along the riverbank where lizards lay in the sun on big paving stones and learned how impossible it was to try and capture one of those tiny, swift creatures.

James celebrated Verona in his work but continued to give Martins Ferry, his boyhood town, hell. Then, as Professor Dougherty points out, he left bitterness behind. Later pieces about Ohio are warm and humorous. In fact, little by little, Ohio began to slip into poems about Italy. James certainly thought of his early home the evening he stood on the bridge over the Adige, in the rain, alone, and "drawled Ohioan."

It was spring the last time we stayed in Verona. One brilliant day we crossed the river and took a long, long walk up a very steep hill on a path which runs next to the old city walls. We ended in the orchard of a small farm. Around us were pear trees in blossom. The ground was covered with new grass and violets. Far below lay Verona caught in a bend of the river.

At the end of James's life the dark city and forest on the shores of the Adige became infused with light. Verona might be a place to die but it was also a place where one could shine, drift like a feather, float. James had moved away from the man who wrote "now I know nothing I can die alone" for he had come to understand "to take a long time to live is to take a long time to understand your life is your own life." He was able to accept the value of his work, the worth of himself and, in quiet triumph, say "I feel like the light of the River Adige."

Anne Wright

About the Author

David C. Dougherty was born in Wheeling, West Virginia. He completed a degree in history and English at West Liberty State College, West Virginia, and did graduate work at Xavier University and Miami University in Ohio. While he was a Woodrow Wilson dissertation fellow, he completed a dissertation on the narrative poetry of Robinson Jeffers.

He taught briefly at Miami University. Currently he is professor of English at Loyola College in Maryland where he was for several years chairman of the English department. He has also taught in the School of Continuing Studies at the Johns Hopkins University. In 1983, he was visiting tutor at St. John's College in Annapolis, Maryland.

His publications have appeared in regional and national journals as well as several reference books. In addition to many essays on James Wright, these include studies of the work of Jeffers, John Updike, Saul Bellow, Raymond Chandler, Walker Percy, Galway Kinnell, John Gardner, and others. He contributes frequently to regional newspapers on environmental, political, and cultural issues.

Preface

Any study of the work of a contemporary writer presents unique challenges, and those challenges grow exponentially with the scope of the work. A brief article may focus on a single interesting aspect of the writer's achievement and may almost ignore historical considerations. In an extended treatment, however, the author's place in literary history becomes an important issue. Contemporary writers have not yet survived the test of history, and our attempts to assess the achievement of a current artist become little more than informed speculation.

James Wright is a contemporary poet, but his work is complete. His untimely death at age 52 silenced a vigorous, powerful voice. It is now time to begin systematically to examine his work in the context of literary history. His reputation among his contemporaries leaves no doubt about his importance to his age. Other writers consistently praise his integrity as a poet and his willingness to take risks in his art. He has figured prominently in the development of three decades of American poetry. Only future generations can decide whether he was an effective writer on current concerns or a poet whose universality and eloquence speak to all ages.

Although I have strong convictions about the ultimate verdict of literary history on Wright, this study makes no extensive attempt to pursue these convictions. It rather attempts to provide the reader with an historical study of Wright's development as a craftsman, so that readers may arrive at their own decisions about his historical importance.

Three principal intentions govern this study. The first is to demonstrate the continuity of Wright's development as an artist and as a man of integrated vision. Because his own style changed twice, and each of those changes was important in the development of contemporary poetry, it is prudent to emphasize the continuity of his vision and technique. This does not deny the historical significance of *The Branch Will Not Break* and *Two Citizens*. The point is that Wright did not shift with current literary fashions. He was growing in individual and integrated artistic vision. Instead of following trends in contemporary poetry, Wright set the tone for new ways to compose poems.

The second goal is to suggest an intended unity in each of Wright's books of poems. Like Yeats and Roethke, Wright was always concerned with the internal dynamics of a collection, and he wanted each volume to add up to something more than the sum of its individual poems. He guided the reader by dividing the early volumes into sections, but with *The Branch Will Not Break* he used more subtle principles of unity. Each major collection includes, for example, one poem about poetry, and the discussion of that poem, early in each chapter, attempts to define certain principles that unify the collection.

The third intention is to provide the reader with useful readings of as many poems as possible. This involves many compromises, for most of Wright's poems are rich enough to invite commentary. Many discussions were reluctantly abandoned as the project developed, and some readers will be disappointed to find scant mention of a favorite poem. I have chosen extended discussion of crucial poems over an attempt to cover everything. Where a critical controversy exists, I have tried briefly to summarize the discussion, rather than to engage in artificial argument with those critics whose views I do not share. An obvious corollary of this procedure is that these readings are not the only possible understandings of Wright's poems. My hope is that readers will study the poems and arrive at readings that reflect their own experience of them.

A portion of this study considers literary influences on Wright. My intention is not to be complete or to work through the implications of each influence in detail. This work will be undertaken by future commentators, but some preliminary discussion of literary influence is included to suggest Wright's immersion in literary tradition.

Discussions of several poems call attention to echoes of the phrasing, style, themes, or strategies of poets Wright admired, including Catullus, Horace, Virgil, Shakespeare, Swift, Wordsworth, Whitman, and many twentieth-century writers. Because of the current revolution against the allusiveness of Eliot and his followers, an unsympathetic reader might infer that Wright is not an original poet. This is not my view. Whether or not one agrees with Eliot's poetics, as Wright surely did not, we must respect Eliot's belief that true originality consists in adding to a vital literary tradition. All but the most flamboyantly irreverent poets pay homage to that tradition by echoing and ultimately assimilating the phrases and concerns of their fellow writers, living and dead.

A poet with a profound and comprehensive appreciation for literature will be judged finally, not by whether he is influenced by others, but by the quality and stature of those who influenced his work. By this standard, Wright fares well. He drew upon the finest and most influential figures in Latin, British, and American literature.

No preface can acknowledge all the assistance that goes into preparing a book, but I want to thank some people who were especially supportive. Loyola College arranged a sabbatical leave, and Dean David Roswell has supported each step of the endeavor. My colleagues in the English department extended themselves to cover my courses and other assignments for a semester. Many members of the staff of the Loyola-Notre Dame Library ably arranged for me to see copies of materials that are no longer in print. Professor William Pratt of Miami University, at whose home I first met Wright in 1969, has encouraged me in my studies of Wright over more than a decade.

Mrs. Anne Wright graciously granted a long interview, read through a draft of the first chapter, and helped me with many biographical details. Mr. John Storck, the director of the Martins Ferry Public Library and an expert on Wright, looked up dates and places efficiently and cheerfully. Professor Peter Stitt of the University of Houston kindly shared information from his research toward the authorized biography and contributed useful comments on one of the more speculative critical issues in chapter four.

A special kind of gratitude is due my children, Jill, Sam, and Carl, who usually understood why they had to be so quiet in their father's study, and to Barbara, who helped explain the need for patience.

David C. Dougherty

Loyola College in Maryland

Acknowledgments

Permission to quote from the following works is gratefully acknowledged here:

From the poetry of James Wright:
Copyright © 1982. Reprinted from *This Journey* by permission of Random House, Inc.
Copyright © 1977. Reprinted from *To a Blossoming Pear Tree* by permission of Farrar, Straus & Giroux, Inc.
Copyright © 1973. Reprinted from *Two Citizens* by permission of Edith Anne Wright.
Copyright © 1971 by James Wright. Reprinted from *Collected Poems* by permission of Wesleyan University Press.

From James and Franz Wright's translation of the work of Herman Hesse. Copyright © 1972. Reprinted from *Wandering* by permission of Farrar, Straus & Giroux, Inc.

From Peter Stitt's interview, "The Art of Poetry XIX: James Wright," *Paris Review* 62 (1975):35–61. Reprinted by permission of *The Paris Review*.

From Dave Smith's interview, "James Wright: The Pure Clear Word, An Interview," in *The Pure Clear Word: Essays on the Poetry of James Wright,* edited by Dave Smith, University of Illinois Press. Copyright © 1982. Reprinted by permission of the Board of Trustees of the University of Illinois.

Chronology

1927 James Arlington Wright born 13 December, the second son of Jessie and Dudley Wright, in Martins Ferry, Ohio.

1946 Graduates from Martins Ferry Senior High School; enlists in United States Army.

1946–1947 Serves tour of Army duty in Japan.

1948 Enters Kenyon College, Gambier, Ohio.

1952 Marries Liberty Kardules, 10 February, in the Greek Orthodox Church in Martins Ferry; completes degree at Kenyon; first poem published in *Western Review;* Fulbright scholar at the University of Vienna.

1953 Son Franz Paul born in Austria in March; begins graduate study at the University of Washington, Seattle.

1954 *The Green Wall* chosen for the Yale Series of Younger Poets.

1957 Accepts teaching appointment at University of Minnesota, Minneapolis; *The Green Wall* published; first important critical essay, "The Stiff Smile of Mr. Warren," appears in *Kenyon Review.*

1958 Initiates contact with Robert Bly; son Marshall born.

1959 *Saint Judas.*

1962 First marriage ends in divorce.

1963 *The Branch Will Not Break;* Afterword for Thomas Hardy's *Far From the Madding Crowd.*

1964 Teaches at Macalester College; translates *The Rider on the White Horse and Selected Stories* by Theodor Storm.

1965 Guggenheim fellowship, travels in California, Ohio, Minnesota, and New York.

1966 Accepts position in English department at Hunter College, New York.

1967 Marries Edith Anne Runk in New York.

1968 *Shall We Gather at the River.*

1970 Selects and translates *Poems* by Hermann Hesse.

1971 *Collected Poems;* fellowship in American Academy of Poets.

1972 Pulitzer Prize for *Collected Poems;* collaborates with son Franz on translation of Hesse's *Wandering;* travels in Europe.

1973 Death of father; *Two Citizens.*

1974 Death of mother; nervous breakdown.

1976 *Moments of the Italian Summer.*

1977 *To a Blossoming Pear Tree.*

1978 Guggenheim fellowship, travels in Europe.

1980 Dies in New York, 25 March.

1981 *The Summers of James and Annie Wright.*

1982 *This Journey.*

Chapter One

The Life and Times of James Wright

Among the American poets who led the contemporary reaction to the kind of poetry perfected by T. S. Eliot, Ezra Pound, and the other great modernists, James Wright occupies a central but unique position. Literary historians, whatever their attitudes toward the revolution in taste that occurred during the 1950s, have recognized Wright as one of the foremost craftsmen among those advocating the new aesthetic. At the same time, Wright was neither polemical nor controversial. He did not write extended defenses of his experimental methods, as did his more vocal contemporaries Robert Bly and Charles Olson. He influenced the new poetry of the decades following World War II primarily by offering the example of a serious and capable craftsman who periodically reexamined his poetics in order to grow as an artist.

This is not to imply that Wright was devoid of theory. By academic training and association, he was a careful and deliberate thinker about the craft and effects of poetry. In his occasional interviews and discussions of fellow writers, he comments perceptively on the craft and discipline of writing. He chose, however, not to associate closely with any of the principal schools of postmodern poetry. Although he has been identified in much of the critical literature with the "surrealist" or "deep image" school that grew up around Bly in Minnesota during the 1960s, this association served Wright as a training period. He needed to revise his attitudes toward poetry, and by experimenting with several of the assumptions Bly explored during the time of their close association, Wright refined his own aims while considering, modifying, and ultimately moving beyond the avenues this school opened for the new poetry.

Wright was a perceptive reader and critic, but he chose not to make his mark as an analyst of the written word. His critical instinct was proved prophetic by his review of Robert Penn Warren's *Promises*, a volume that has since been acknowledged by literary historians as a breakthrough in the development of postmodern poetry. In 1958, long before academic critics recognized the importance of Warren's new direction, Wright said: "a major writer at the height of his fame has chosen, not to write his good poems over again, but to break his own rules, to shatter his words and try to recreate them, to fight through and beyond his own craftsmanship in order to revitalize his language at the sources of tenderness and horror."[1] This exceptionally perceptive judgment has been confirmed by scholars, and the implications Wright saw in Warren's change have become central to our understanding of developments in poetry since 1958.

When Wright mentioned contemporary writers, he was almost always supportive and sympathetic. He has praised the efforts of many well-known poets as well as more obscure writers like John Hall Wheelock, H. Phelps Putnam, and Bill Knott. He commends his fellow writers' honesty, directness of feeling, willingness to attempt new forms, and integrity of craft. These are, of course, the qualities Wright sought in his own poems.

Wright censured only a few writers. One is John Updike, whom Wright often associates with successful commercial writers. In one of his more playful moments, he says, "[i]t was obvious that I cannot hope to be a prose stylist like, say, Harold Robbins, Jacquelin Susann, Faith Baldwin, or even John Updike."[2] In "Lament: Fishing with Richard Hugo," Wright makes fun of Updike again:

> If John Updike had been
> Ed Bedford, . . .
> Ed's dank tavern might have become
> The Puce Nook, featuring
> A menu illuminated by Doris Day,
> With Updike composing the prose
> Of Howard Johnson, accompanying himself
> On an oboe, singing of tender
> Succulent golden
> French fries.[3]

This witty selection tells us indirectly what Wright valued in his poems. Updike is accused of transforming the grubby charm of Bedford's bar into an antiseptic, standardized, but characterless environment. Wright prefers the honesty of Bedford's tawdry bar, where Ed overcharged the fishermen, over all the perfect but hollow franchises in the civilized world. He wants a literary style that is direct, rather than a display of verbal cleverness in which real feeling is lost in glittering surfaces. He prefers an art that captures the authentic and idiosyncratic charm of Bedford's to one that celebrates, with whatever lyricism, the standardization of American life.

Wright also condemns writers who imitate current literary fashions without developing the discipline to control their expression. In "Many of Our Waters: Variations on a Poem by a Black Child," one of Wright's artistic professions of belief is prefaced by a scathing comment on undisciplined and imitative poets:

> The young poets of New York come to me with
> Their mangled figures of speech,
> But they have little pity
> For the pure clear word.[4]

The "pure clear word" became Wright's artistic credo. These poets deny that premise so basic to his poetry because they are more concerned with technical dexterity than with substance. In the early essay on Warren, Wright included himself among the poets who substitute fashion for craft. He said that Warren's failures are worth "more than the ten thousand safe and competent versifyings produced by our current crop of punks in America. I am spared the usual but boring critical courtesy of mentioning names by the fact that we all know who we are" (648). He later identifies himself directly with "us safe boys" (648). It is clear from these objections to various types of literary escapism and retreats from reality covered by clever surfaces that the elements Wright valued most in art are directness, authenticity, honesty, and discipline.

These are the elements that have caused a few critics to raise questions about Wright's own work. The risk one always runs when either integrity or sincerity is offered as a primary aesthetic value is that one will be accused of sentimentality. Wright's poems have risked the direct statement and have occasionally been charged with sentimentality or solipsism. But even when there have been doubts about his poetry, there has been agreement that it is a central expression of the contemporary revolution in taste. Much more frequently, Wright's poems are held forth as examples of what is best in contemporary American poetry.

An Ohio Native

James Arlington Wright was born in Martins Ferry, Ohio, on 13 December 1927. This was before the Great Depression, but that disaster would dominate the youth of this boy from the industrial Ohio River basin. The compassion and economic insecurity that characterize so many of Wright's poems probably have their roots in the financial catastrophe. The depression affected the entire country, but economic hardships are particularly felt in a region dependent on heavy industry, where the whole financial structure relies on large orders coming in to huge, impersonal mills and factories.

James was the second of three sons of Dudley and Jessie Wright. The three boys and their older sister Margie grew up in a blue-collar community. Jessie Wright left school to work in a laundry and later married Dudley. The husband, also having dropped out of school in order to become a wage earner, spent fifty years working for a glass factory. As James would write later, "one slave / To Hazel-Atlas Glass became my father. / He tried to teach me kindness" (*CP,* 82). Some of Wright's finest poems treat the tender feelings he had toward his father, who remained kind although he "wrestled and mastered great machines" and even "broke stones" to support his family. By material standards, the Wright family certainly was not well off. By the more important standards of love and shared experience, however, they had what seems to have been a good life in a bad place during a hard time.

The valley in which the Wrights lived provided a provocative setting for the boy who would mature as a poet torn between love and contempt for his native place. Then, as now, it was a study in contrasts. Natural beauty is everywhere. Steep hills rise from the river valley, and the bright green of hardwood and pine trees shimmers in the sun. Fertile, productive farmlands punctuate the hillsides. In the midst of this beauty, the land bears brutal scars of human rapacity. Strip mines, relatively shallow cuts in the ground to extract minerals, usually coal, mar the landscape. Many have not yet been reclaimed and leave angry gashes in the hillsides.

The basin bears other marks of human greed. Steel mills, belching out dirty smoke and oxidizing themselves and everything near them, occupy the center of such cities as Weirton, Steubenville, and Wheeling (West Virginia). The river itself, though Wright speaks of swimming from Martins Ferry to the northwest corner of Wheeling Island, was becoming polluted with industrial and residential waste. In an autobiographical note, Wright remembers that an "open sewer from Martins Ferry poured into the river about a mile upstream; and, a little further up, such factories as Wheeling Steel, Laughlin Steel and the Blaw-Knox Company were constantly presenting their modest contributions on which the health of the American economy continue {*sic*} to depend."[5]

Dudley Wright's fortunes were better than those of many of his contemporaries. He was at least never fired from his job; instead he was subjected to that insidious expedient of heavy industry, the lay-off. Often he was simply told not to return to work until further notice. The family must have struggled to adjust to such uncertainty. The late prose-poem "Honey" recalls a fight between Dudley and his son-in-law Paul, and James interprets the fight as motivated by economic stress: "They were fighting with each other because one strong man, a factory worker, was laid off from his work, and the other strong man, the driver of a coal truck, was laid off from his work" (*TJ*, 82). James was always sympathetic with, perhaps a bit sentimental about, those who suffer economic hardship.

Economic worries aside, the Wrights seem to have lived normal American lives in an industrial setting. James explored regions forbidden by his parents; he tells stories about railroad detectives, tramps, neighborhood grouches, treacherous suck-holes, and the pipe where the sewer was allowed to spill into the river.

When he was not discovering forbidden places, he went to the public schools in Martins Ferry. Two teachers, Elizabeth Willerton Esterly and Helen McNeely Sheriff, made a powerful impression on James by rescuing him from a vocational program and introducing him to Latin poetry and the Russian writers.[6] The impression made by Latin works remains in the mature poetry, especially in the author's devotion to Horace and Catullus. The Russian influence is more difficult to define, but "In Shame and Humiliation" uses an epigraph from Dostoyevsky's *Notes from the Underground,* and the mood of many poems reflects the great Russian writers' concerns with guilt, the problems of brotherhood, and the dark side of human experience. At the least, we can guess that the influence of Esterly and Sheriff opened up to the young Wright an alternative to the lives of quiet desperation he saw among some of his family circle and acquaintances living in the industrial basin of the Ohio River.

World War II brought the United States out of the Great Depression, and young Wright left the Ohio valley for the first time. Upon completing high school in 1946, he enlisted in the Army. He was stationed briefly in the Engineers' School in Fort Belvoir, Virginia; then he served with the occupation forces in Japan, where he learned to love the lifestyle and the terse, controlled literature. For the rest of his life, he remembered fondly the kindness and forgiveness he found among the people of a vanquished nation.

Out of the service, Wright became the first member of his family to attend college, and the college he chose—or, as he once put it, the college that accepted him—was Kenyon, in western Ohio. Many competent poets and teachers were on the faculty, like Philip Timberlake, whose kindness and generosity to Wright, both personal and professional, were rewarded when Wright dedicated *Saint Judas* to him. He is probably the subject of "At the Grave." John Crowe Ransom, with whom Wright took one course, was synonymous with literary excellence at Kenyon. Before he completed his degree in 1952, Wright had won the Robert Frost Poetry Prize.

James married Liberty Kardules, a classmate at Martins Ferry High School, the daughter of a contractor, and a student of nursing, on 10 February 1952. Shortly afterward, an equally momentous change occurred in the Wrights' life. James was chosen as a Fulbright scholar at the University of Vienna, where he studied the fiction of Theodor Storm, a volume of which he would later translate.

Vienna was a cosmpolitan center, almost an exact opposite of provincial Martins Ferry. Everywhere Wright found art, music, and lively conversation. He loved the opera, the open-air concerts, and the art galleries. The stay exhilirated and enlightened the young poet, but he did not achieve the expatriate status of Eliot and Henry James because Fulbrights, like all good things, come to an end. His son Franz, however, was born in Vienna in March 1953.

Upon returning to America, Wright entered the University of Washington, where he took a traditional program in English. He fondly remembered courses in medieval and eighteenth-century literature, and a creative writing course with Theodore Roethke, who influenced the direction of his work profoundly. They remained friends and corresponded until Roethke's death in 1963. Beatrice Roethke, the subject of "On a Hostess Saying Good Night," visited the Wrights in New York several years after Theodore's death. Wright completed his M.A. by writing a book of poems. In 1959 he defended a doctoral dissertation entitled "The Comic Imagination of the Young Dickens."

His academic progress was complemented by his growing recognition as a poet. His first published poem, "Villanelle for the New Soldiers," appeared in *Western Review* in 1952. By 1957, thirty-three poems had been printed in magazines, from regional journals to national and international ones like *Poetry,* the *Paris Review,* and *Harper's.* In 1954, his collection *The Green Wall* was chosen by W. H. Auden to receive the annual Yale Series of Younger Poets award.

In 1957 the Wrights moved to Minneapolis. Now a member of the English department at the University of Minnesota, Wright continued to write poems and worked on a study of Dickens. Another son, Marshall, was born in 1958, and in the next year *Saint Judas* came out. All was not well with Dr. and Mrs. Wright, however, despite the many recognitions his achievements had received. The poet felt that he had reached a dead end with *Saint Judas* and publicly stated that he would never again write poetry in the same mode. In addition to this frustration about his art, he was not entirely happy with his academic position or the midwestern city. In a letter to Roethke, he complained that Minneapolis "looks as socially bleak as it is physically attractive," and in another, he compared Seattle with "some impossible Eden." Asking Robert Heilman to consider his application for a post at Washington, he wrote, "Minneapolis is okay, I guess, as midwestern cities go. But I find the best of midwestern cities somewhat offensive."[7] His despair at the inadequacy of midwestern culture is recorded in one of his most despondent works, "The Minneapolis Poem."

His marriage was also failing; he and Liberty agreed to separate several times between 1959 and their eventual divorce in 1962. His anguish is recorded in "Having Lost My Sons, I confront the Wreckage of the Moon: Christmas, 1960":

> I am sick
> Of it, and I go on,
> Living, alone, alone,
> Past the charred silos, past the hidden graves
> Of Chippewas and Norwegians. . . .
> And I am lost in the beautiful white ruins
> Of America.
>
> (*CP,* 131–32).

Many poems of the period share this mood of total isolation and the sense that personal anguish reflects a failure to become a vital part of the culture. He wrote Heilman in 1959 that his personal life was "in

a state bordering on chaos," that he and Liberty had decided they
were not compatible, and that "[i]t is not pleasant for me to face the
fact that, whatever I may be as a writer, I am a flat failure as a human
being," a charge Heilman gently reprimanded in his reply.[8]

While the personal crisis raged, his writing actually improved. He
undertook a complete revision of his poetic practice and finished in
1963 one of the most important books in American poetry since
World War II, *The Branch Will Not Break*. The next year, while he
was teaching at Macalester College in St. Paul on a leave of absence,
his application for tenure at Minnesota was denied. Because Macalester welcomed his continued presence, this decision had little effect on
his academic career, but it was a personal and professional disappointment.

The most pleasant part of Wright's stay in Minnesota was his association with Robert and Carol Bly. He wrote Robert Bly a sixteen-
page letter in 1958 and received an invitation to Odin House. At
Bly's farm, Wright passed many pleasant afternoons discussing poetry, Latin American poets, the translation process, and the revolution Bly was leading through his small press the *Fifties*. Wright tells
the charming story of Carol's locking him up in a chicken house the
Blys had converted as a study in order to force him to complete an
essay for the *Sixties* and to prevent him from getting drunk.

By this time, alcohol had complicated the many personal problems
Wright was having: "I remember those afternoons in the chicken
house as a curious combination of a pleasant study, Yaddo, and
Devil's Island."[9] At the farm, Wright was able to communicate with
nature and the many domesticated animals the Blys kept, in ways
that refreshed his sagging spirits. One of the more charming moments in his books, a blank page entitled "In Memory of the Horse
David, Who Ate One of My Poems," refers to a sway-backed palo-
mino the Blys kept as well as to the blank chapters eighteen and nine-
teen in the ninth volume of one of his favorite novels, Sterne's
Tristram Shandy. At Odin House, he formed lasting friendships with
James Dickey, Donald Hall, Louis Simpson, and John Logan.

In 1965, a Guggenheim fellowship permanently rescued Wright
from Minnesota. He spent the year visiting his former teacher Elizabeth Esterly and his sons in California, the Blys in Minnesota, and
his parents in Ohio. He had not resolved all his personal problems,
but he felt that Minneapolis was behind him, and he worked steadily
on a new book, *Shall We Gather at the River*. The following year, he

moved to New York to teach at Hunter College. He soon became a full professor, a position he held for the rest of his life. At Hunter, he enjoyed a reputation as a conscientious and gifted teacher. In an era when the academy became the patron of poets, Wright refused to teach creative writing. He once told a class at the University of Illinois, "I'm a teacher by profession, not a writer . . . in fact, I don't even teach poetry." Distrusting the workshops in poetry that were very popular during the 1970s, Wright preferred to offer traditional courses, particularly one in the English novel in which he could teach his beloved Dickens and Hardy and a genre course in comedy that featured Cervantes, Sterne, and Swift. He reaffirmed his professional commitment when he told a former pupil, "I've written books of verse, but I'm a professor. And to me personally, teaching is the art that gives me the more pleasure. I'm not trying to put myself down as a poet, but I mean what I say."[10] At Hunter he also came to know fellow poet Galway Kinnell, whose friendship and support were of critical importance.

In 1967, Wright married Edith Anne Runk, a nursery school director and educator, whom he had met after a reading by Josephine Miles on 29 April 1966. This second marriage helped to resolve many of his personal problems. Anne became an inspiration as well as a partner. A photograph of one of her sculptures adorns *Collected Poems;* her poem "Little Marble Boy" appears in *To a Blossoming Pear Tree;* and she wrote four of the prose pieces in *The Summers of James and Annie Wright.* The Wrights traveled frequently in Europe, Hawaii, the American southwest, and Canada. Their trips to Europe in 1970 and 1972 revived the love James had felt for the place during the Vienna year, but his renewed imagination was fired more by the countrysides and cities of Italy and France than by Austria. An extended trip was cut short by the death of his father in 1973. His mother died several months later, and James's grief brought on a nervous breakdown.

A later trip to Europe, made possible by a second Guggenheim fellowship in 1978, proved wonderful yet disappointing. Anne reports that James was distressed by the "Americanization" of his beloved Italy. He now saw vandalism and extensive drug use there, and some of the tenderness he had felt before was replaced by frustration. An anecdote from the last trip illustrates Wright's sense of humor and generosity of spirit. Driving through Tuscany, they were told by Anne's sister Jane about the Madonna of Carda. Jane had read in

H. V. Morton's *A Traveler in Italy* about soldiers who had vowed to bring home to Carda a statue of Mary they found in a ruined church during one of the Tuscan wars. It proved to be one of the most exquisite of Andrea Della Robbia's Marys. When they saw a road sign that said "Carda, Madonna Della Robbia," James remarked that the Carda Chamber of Commerce must have read Morton. After a long drive through the mountains, the travelers found Carda, but when Anne asked for directions, the women in the shop wept and told her the madonna had been "rubata," or stolen a few years before. As they drove away, James exploded, "It's all they had! The bastards!"[11]

Now settled as both a husband and a poet, Wright enjoyed the prizes and awards that came rapidly. He received a fellowship from the American Academy of Poets in 1971 and won major awards from the Poetry Society of America (1972), *Poetry* magazine (1968), and Brandeis Unviersity (1970). His *Collected Poems* won a Pulitzer Prize in 1972. He was in constant demand on the lecture circuit and participated in a celebration of the visit of Pablo Neruda, whose poems he had translated, to New York. In January 1980, he was invited to a White House reception for poets and commented on the pride Dudley and Jessie Wright would have felt in knowing that a poet from Martins Ferry had been invited to meet a president.

The Wrights returned from their last trip to Europe in September 1979. James had noticed a painful and chronic sore throat while in Paris; in December, his illness was diagnosed as cancer of the tongue. With the threat of death, which he had both courted and feared throughout his literary life, now imminent, Wright completed pieces for *The Summers of James and Annie Wright*. He entered the hospital a week after the White House reception. When Kinnell visited James in the hospital on 17 March, Wright gave him a photocopy of the manuscript of *This Journey* and wrote on his copy, "I think the book is more or less done." Eight days later, on 25 March 1980, James Wright died.

Three Major Influences

A complete account of the literary influences on James Wright's poetry is beyond the scope of this study. Like any important poet, Wright was a product of the works he read, appreciated, and absorbed. He loved to quote long passages from a variety of poets at a moment's inspiration, and he often copied poems by others simply to get a feel for their rhythm and style. It will help us understand important developments in Wright's work, however, if we consider briefly the influence of three fellow poets whom Wright knew and worked with during his own development as a craftsman, especially because they provide a capsule history of American poetry in the twentieth century.

John Crowe Ransom was a literary giant by the time Wright enrolled in his course at Kenyon. He was a famous poet, a leader of the Agrarian school of social and economic thought in southern American literature, and one of the founding fathers of the New Criticism. By 1948, Ransom had written five important books of poetry, two controversial studies of social issues, and an important treatise on criticism. He also edited one of the most influential journals in America, the *Kenyon Review,* in which he encouraged the publication of a certain type of well-made poem and the discussion of current issues in literary theory.

Ransom must have been a genteel but intimidating example for a young writer just returned from the service. Wright spoke in 1979 about his impression of Ransom as a splendid teacher because he was a magnificent reader of poems. Studying under Ransom did not involve writing original works, but did require that the pupil understand the architectonics of many of the best poems in English. For Wright, the chief value imparted by Ransom was his understanding "that humility is a necessary intellectual virtue, leaving its moral virtue aside. He tried to instill in us the recognition of how necessary it is to pay humble attention to what an author is trying to say. . . . [I]n Ortega's sense, Ransom was a noble man, as distinguished from a barbarian. . . . He could be extremely funny. His genuine humility had quite a striking effect on students, in our occasional arrogance."[12] Wright considered Ransom a mentor who understood the relation between poetry and criticism in the manner of Aristotle, Coleridge, and Johnson; he once quoted Robert Lowell's comment that Ransom was "the best conversationalist alive in the United States."[13]

Wright of course knew Ransom's poems well. Ransom's penchant for writing mini-elegies on inconsequential subjects like a dead boy in Virginia or Janet's hen certainly stayed with Wright, though he could have absorbed similar inclinations from other acknowledged masters like Robinson or Hardy. Wright, too, would write brief elegies for the unfortunate and the unknown, including the prostitute Jenny, his uncle Willy Lyons, an ancient, obscure Chinese politician,

American Indians named Little Crow and Red Jacket, President
Harding, the rapist Caryl Chessman, and the local murderer George
Doty.

Wright was probably also influenced, especially in his early poems,
by Ransom's use of controlled meters and surprising rhymes, although these devices too could have been learned from Robinson,
Hardy, or Robert Frost and reinforced by the achievements of
Wright's contemporaries, especially Richard Wilbur and W. S. Merwin. Surely the intricate rhyming effects in poems like "Arrangements with Earth for Three Dead Friends," using iambic pentameter
in a rhyme scheme *a b c d e e d c b a,* or "Evening," employing trimeter lines in a seven-stanza arrangement rhyming *a b a c c b d d,* owe
some of their technical complexity to a master Wright knew while he
was learning to write.

A force from the old school of modern poetry, Ransom was an influence Wright, like other young poets of the 1950s, would need to
assimilate in order to discard. Wright was never comfortable with, or
terribly good at, the kinds of irony and verbal wit that characterize
Ransom's best poems. With his fastidiously playful elegance, Ransom
creates an impersonal and detached attitude Wright never sought in
his own art. Wright seldom used irony and impersonality, as Ransom
did, to write himself out of the poem. Even while he reflected Ransom's intricate patterns of sound, he sought a directness of address
foreign to both the New Criticism and the kind of poem Ransom
wrote and praised.

When Wright went to graduate school, he studied with a master
from the first generation of contemporary poets, Theodore Roethke.
Although Wright took only one course in creative writing with
Roethke, they remained friends and correspondents. Wright referred
to Roethke as someone who "was always stimulating, and he was such
a genuine poet. He really couldn't have been anything else. He was
one of the chosen ones, I think."[14] In a letter that discusses Wright's
discomfort with the kind of poetry he had printed in *The Green Wall,*
he tells his mentor, "I think you are not only a great poet but also
something even more important—a heroic human being."[15] Roethke
is one of the "two Teds" to whom *The Green Wall* is dedicated; the
other is James's older brother.

Roethke had broken with one central assumption of modern poetry
by celebrating his origins in the romantic tradition. Rather than
write the kind of objective, self-contained artifacts Ransom preferred,

Roethke made his soul, tormented and joyful as it alternately was, the principal subject of his art. Roethke saw his poems, not as detached and self-contained units of artistic meaning, but as expressions of his own intuitive consciousness in such meditative poems as "The Lost Son" and "The Shape of the Fire." When he risked self-disclosure, he used images that connect at preconscious levels with the reader. His poems create, like those of Blake or Yeats, a private system of symbols and meanings. Occasionally the associations demanded by the figurative language seem arbitrary to the reader unfamiliar with the larger context of Roethke's works. This would be true also of some of the poetry Wright produced in his mature years. In both poets, this mildly defiant attitude toward the communicative purpose of figurative language represents a radical departure from the kind of objective image perfected by the modern poets and encouraged by the formalist criticism that had come to dominate literary and academic circles.

While Wright studied with him, Roethke alternated between tightly controlled lyrics employing complex stanza forms and intricate rhyme, like "Four for Sir John Davies" or "I Knew a Woman," and open forms, in which the subject alone determines the line, such as "The Shape of the Fire" or "Meditations of an Old Woman." At the time of Wright's stay in Washington, then, he would be encouraged in the tightly controlled poetry he had already written and influenced toward the more open or organic form he would soon learn to write, by a mentor who was writing excellent poems in both modes during the same period. Wright summarized Roethke's influence by saying, "He taught mainly the craft, and he . . . was an entirely conscious craftsman. . . . And Roethke understood that it is careful, conscious craft which liberates your feelings and liberates your imagination."[16]

Another critical influence on Wright was Robert Bly, with whom he worked closely in Minnesota. Always more a theoretician than Wright, Bly vigorously advocated a new kind of poetry. In his little magazine the *Fifties,* which changed its name with each new decade, Bly argued, often stridently, for a poetry that would take its energy from unconscious or archetypal imagery. In 1966 Bly, under the pseudonym "Crunk," wrote an introduction to Wright's work in which he praises Wright as one of a few poets to break away from the "moral and philosophical" reasoning that, Bly believes, has inhibited American and English poetry for many years.[17]

Bly adamantly rejected the popular well-made poem of the decades following the decline of literary modernism. He felt that such poems were artificial. In their place Bly advocated a poetry of commitment. He campaigned against American involvement in Vietnam and enlisted such poets as Wright and Kinnell in an effort to fuse art and social action, American Writers Against the Vietnam War. Wright vigorously lent his voice to the movement. Bly insisted that the poet has a moral responsibility to speak out on issues of the day. Beginning with his watershed poem "At the Executed Murderer's Grave," Wright would often use his artistic voice to address contemporary issues directly and unambiguously.

More important to Wright's technical development was his introduction by Bly to the Spanish and Latin American poets. Always an avid translator, Bly was convinced that the future of American poetry depended on immediate assimilation of these influences. The best way to absorb these would be to translate—in the manner prescribed years before by Ezra Pound—the originals into English: to interact creatively with the poems and to value capturing the spirit of the original over fidelity to the prose sense of the poem. Often collaborating with Bly or members of his circle, Wright translated poems by Pablo Neruda, Cesar Vallejo, Jorge Guillen, Juan Ramon Jiminez, and Pedro Salinas. He returned to the German to translate Trakl and Goethe. From these poets, especially Trakl, whose imagery influenced Wright profoundly, he learned to use surreal imagery. This kind of image had lurked in the background of the early poems, but Trakl and the Spanish American poets provided examples by which Wright could confidently explore the implications of his intuition. He told an interviewer how both Bly and translation affected him: "Robert Bly suggested to me that there is a kind of poetry that can be written. People have written it in some other languages. He said it might be possible to come back to our own language through reading them and translating them, and I think that in one sense this has been the value of translation."[18] The example of Neruda, the legislator-poet of Chile, reinforced Bly's aim of writing an activist poetry employing surreal and archetypal imagery.

This involvement with poetry in other languages led Bly and Wright toward a new American surrealism, which found its local voice as the "deep image." While it is a popular oversimplification to identify Wright with the deep imagists, it is necessary to understand some attitudes associated with this school in order to see how Wright developed his unique imagery. Bly and Robert Kelly, the editor of

Trobar magazine, felt that the greatest achievement of Spanish American poetry was its use of imagery to bear the exclusive burden of meaning in a poem. This is not at all like the imagist school of the first decades of this century, for the deep imagists, influenced by Jung as much as by Neruda, sought through poetry a direct access to the unconscious rather than an impressionistic rendering of surface phenomena. The image gathers force within the unconscious and connects with the reader on equally unconscious levels. These poets were not concerned with exploring the motives for their behavior, as were the confessional poets of the same period, but with forging links between unconscious and conscious levels of experience.

Although the deep imagists were never a formal group like the Black Mountain school in North Carolina, scattered poets at the inception of the movement shared a belief in the primacy of authentic imagery, which in turn depends on the honesty and sincerity of the poet, over complex literary techniques. As Charles Molesworth claims, one premise of the deep image school nearly proposes a type of automatic writing as an artistic goal; the individual poet becomes almost a passive medium through whom images charged with archetypal significance emerge—something remotely akin to Coleridge's concept of the Aeolian harp. What Molesworth calls the "subjective image" is "produced by the workings of the transrational mind, charged with mythical resonances, and bearing the major responsibility for organizing the poem's energies. This image . . . resulted more from a special gathering of consciousness than from any purely verbal manipulation; it came from a region beyond syntax, and it had powers more than grammatical. To write such poetry, one needed a carefully plotted surrender, and to read it required a discipline less passive than deeply meditative."[19]

As the earlier critical movement toward formalism supported Wright's inclination to follow Ransom's leads, the evolution of archetypal criticism encouraged him to move in the direction of self-exploration suggested by Roethke and toward the deep image proposed by Bly. By the time Wright associated with Bly, many implications of Northrop Frye's *Anatomy of Criticism* (1957) were being explored by an academic community weary of the rigorous reading without personal involvement promoted by the formalists. While critics were looking for unconscious patterns with collective significance in works of art, it was natural for poets who had tired of the "autotelic" poem admired by the new critics to seek a new avenue of

expression, and this critical emphasis on the signification of unconscious patterns of imagery corresponded nicely with the kind of poems
Bly and Wright found the Spanish and Latin American poets writing.

Despite these parallels, Wright consistently denied that his poems
exhibit any surrealistic intention. In 1975, he disassociated himself
from the surrealist school with a typical overstatement that his works
"are not surrealistic, they are Horatian and classical. When they
sound surrealistic, all that means is that my attempt to be clear has
failed. They are not surrealistic and I am not a surrealist."[20] "Against
Surrealism" makes a witty case for the rationality of certain "tiny obvious details in human life that survive the divine purpose of boring
fools to death" (*TJ*, 18). Despite these disclaimers, Wright's poems
often exhibit sudden, nonrepresentational, and sometimes arbitrary
imagery like that of the deep imagists and the American surrealists.
Familiar examples include:

> Our father,
> Last evening I devoured the wing
> Of a cloud.
> ("Confession to J. Edgar Hoover," *CP*, 163)

> Many American women mount long stairs
> In the shafts of houses,
> Fall asleep, and suddenly emerge into tottering palaces.
> ("Miners," *CP*, 119)

Can the claims of critics that Wright is a surrealist and a deep image poet be reconciled with those of the poet that he is not? It is true
that, like the deep imagists, Wright uses images that have apparently
arbitrary significance and transrational association. Yet these images
seldom control the central meaning or organization of the poem.
These depend in large measure on a tension between the nonrational
or imperfectly understood object and the alienated speaker. Surrealistic images evoke Wright's main concerns, the alienation of modern
human beings from the world we inhabit and the difficulty of bridg-
ing the gap between the self and what is around us. The universality
sought by the deep imagists is certainly present in Wright's poems,
but this universality is actually communicated to the reader on a rational level. We as readers participate in the poet's anger and despair
at not being able to bring the world to coherence, and in his arbitrary
and seemingly surreal images we experience the shock of recognizing
our own alienation from the processes of nature or society.

Through his associations with these three poets, Wright made his journey to selfhood and authenticity as an artist. This is not to say that other writers did not have an impact on his life and work in important ways. Certainly Walt Whitman, that seminal American bard, was a powerful and formative influence, as were Frost and Robinson. He admired the Roman poets Catullus and Horace and responded to Dickens in ways mentioned in the biographical section of this chapter. He proposed "devotion to Hardy" as a standard for young American poets in a review written while he was preparing *Saint Judas:* "A devotion to Hardy means, among other things, a devotion to an unpretentious style and a willingness to experiment within the very severe confines of traditional lyrical forms."[21] Two of his most moving tributes are "At Thomas Hardy's Birthplace, 1953" and "Lighting a Candle for W. H. Auden." The many writers he translated left formative impressions, the most important from Trakl and Neruda.

The three poets treated here, however, associated directly with Wright during his lifetime, and their impact can be seen as a paradigm for the development of his craft. This development will be a central concern of the next chapters because it is not only the story of one poet's growth, but an important chapter in the history of American poetry since World War II.

Chapter Two

"The Beautiful Language of My Friends": *The Green Wall* and *Saint Judas*

Although his first two volumes received honors, awards, and the immediate respect of his fellow poets, Wright did not long remain satisfied with this achievement. Biographical evidence suggests that he was unhappy with these poems because he felt that they were imitative works by Robinson, Frost, and Hardy. In fact, the dust jacket cover for *The Branch Will Not Break* contains a famous if overstated rejection of Wright's early poems. He says, "Whatever I write from now on will be completely different. I don't know what it will be, but I am finished with what I was doing in that book *{Saint Judas}*."

A restless poet like Wright may overstate the case against his own poems, especially those he wants to move beyond. Poets frequently use violent language to reject their past writing in order to prepare themselves for steps that seem at the time more radical than history will prove them. Such is the case with Wright's first two books. They are neither a sufficient foundation for a reputation as one of the major postwar American poets nor as juvenile or imitative as Wright came to think they were.

If Wright's judgment about the early work proves hyperbolic, critics offer conflicting evaluations. Some, like Henry Taylor and Madeline DeFrees, consider certain poems in the first two books among the best Wright has written, whereas others, like James Breslin and William Matthews, find the early poems too imitative or restricted by an imperfectly suited form, so much so that the poems are of interest primarily because they were written by the poet who would evolve to write *The Branch Will Not Break*.[1] Both judgments seem too extreme to be satisfactory. The early poems are not interesting merely because they are apprentice work; many have lasting aesthetic and emotional value, and it is no accident that several of the most anthologized among Wright's poems come from the first two books. While we should respect early poems as accomplishments in themselves, we must also recognize that they lack the authority and rhetorical distinction of the mature work.

Criticism of Wright's work has customarily defined the stylistic changes that occurred between *Saint Judas* and *The Branch Will Not Break* as a radical breakthrough in technique, but the poet himself consistently denied that his sudden growth represented an artistic conversion. He certainly developed confidence and precision as he matured, but as Taylor has pointed out, he never completely abandoned the formal devices of the early books.[2] His themes remained fairly constant, especially when we consider that his career spanned more than a quarter of a century, and while he used open forms more frequently in the later poems, he never entirely repudiated the basic iambic line or the strategic use of rhyme.

A balanced view of the early poems would evaluate them as sound, intelligent applications of a current aesthetic. They are controlled by formal and traditional devices, but the vision is distinctively Wright's own and is entirely consistent with the vision of the mature work. When he collected his poems in 1971, he kept all but five of the poems from *The Green Wall* and printed *Saint Judas* in its entirety. This in itself indicates that he did not intend to repudiate the early poems. He felt that they were worth preserving, but not worth repeating. He would later make virtually the same statement about his major volumes.

The Revolt against Modernism

The decade during which Wright and other poets of his generation began to write, the 1950s, was characterized by several diverse movements toward new styles. The Beat poets, with Allen Ginsberg and later Lawrence Ferlinghetti as their most vigorous spokesmen, took inspiration from William Blake, Walt Whitman, Ezra Pound, and William Carlos Williams. The Beats tried to forge an aesthetic that would lead to directness and inspiration as the source of poetic truth. Also drawing on Williams and Pound, the Black Mountain school, led by Charles Olson and Robert Creeley, promoted projective verse as a style that accommodated the rhythms of American speech. Robert Lowell, W. D. Snodgrass, and Sylvia Plath began to explore the potential of confessional autobiography as a poetic subject during the later years of the decade.

What all these groups had in common was a desire to escape the powerful authority of the great modern poets. The shadow of Eliot and his school loomed over American poets, but the younger ones did not want merely to echo the voices of the past generation. This need not to repeat was complicated by the fact that the masters of the modernist school were alive in person as well as in their verse and criticism. In 1950, Eliot, Pound, Williams, Ransom, Tate, Moore, Jeffers, and Stevens were still writing, providing reference points for what a modern poem should be. Stanley Kunitz, writing in 1967, recalls that "it was difficult to be taken seriously" as a poet in the shadow of a "dynasty of extraordinary gifts and powers," especially one that exhibited such a "stubborn capacity for survival"[3] as well as artistic excellence. All the schools of poetry during the 1950s reacted against the discontinuous, allusive, densely textured poetry Eliot, his followers, and his imitators had made almost institutional by the end of the Second World War.

This type of poem, with its metaphysical intensity, had been supported by the establishment of formalist criticism in American academies during the previous decade. With its insistence on the close reading of a complex text, formalism had elevated ambiguity, paradox, and allusiveness to the stature of poetic orthodoxy. These strategies acquired the authority that rhyme and conventional meter had until the present century. The younger poets wanted to find a different way to write, a way that would replace autonomy with relevance, objectivity with involvement, dispassionate intellectualism with felt human emotion.

While Wright studied at Kenyon, one important reaction against modernism was making an impact in the small presses. This school, with which Wright was productively if temporarily aligned, may be called the new academic poets. Among the young poets working in this mode were Richard Wilbur, Snodgrass, Galway Kinnell, Anthony Hecht, and W. S. Merwin. All save Wilbur would abandon these methods for more open forms during the next decades.

The reaction of these academic poets was neither as violent nor as polemical as that of the Beats or the Black Mountain school. They tried to remodel rather than demolish the orthodoxy of modern poetry. They resisted the discontinuity, allusiveness, and studied obscurity of many modern poets. They also avoided multilingual poems in the mode of Pound and Eliot. Yet they conformed in the main with the principle that a poem should be objective and intellectual, rather than personal and emotional. The academic poets constructed crisp, self-contained lyrics that differed from their predecessors in scope and accessibility.

Their poems also differed in formal regularity. The revolution was more reactionary than radical in matters of technique. Poets were encouraged to control their material by means of traditional forms. Wit and precision were enhanced by iambic regularity and patterned rhyme. An intellectual satisfaction for the readers of these poems would be to discover new possibilities for communication within conventional forms. To achieve these ends, the academic poets of the decade fused the principles of objectivity and autonomy of the poem with the pastoral tradition of Robinson and Frost. Wright, whose first books conform in important ways with the directions taken by the academic poets, openly acknowledged both Frost and Robinson as influences behind *The Green Wall*.

The Green Wall

In part because it was consistent in style and tone with the practices of the best academic poets, Wright's first collection was honored by being accepted for publication in the Yale Series of Younger Poets, upon the judgment of the most influential poet-critic to succeed Eliot. W. H. Auden clearly felt that these poems deserved recognition. He wrote a perceptive and even prophetic foreword for the collection. Ready to back up his judgment by taking on the labor of critical commentary, Auden provides the first significant discussion of Wright's poems to reach print.

Auden has surprisingly little to say about technical aspects of the poems, but he comments perceptively on Wright's modernity, or the degree to which his themes reflect the existential condition of modern humanity and the poetic possibilities of that condition. He points out Wright's tendency to identify with the unwanted and the outcasts of modern society and discusses profound cultural implications of that identification. He sees it as symptomatic of a modern tendency to distrust persons who have achieved public fame or esteem. In a comment that has proved prophetic, Auden observes, "the persons who have stimulated Mr. Wright's imagination include a lunatic, a man who has failed to rescue a boy from drowning, a murderer, a lesbian, a prostitute, a police informer, and some children, one of them deaf. Common to them all is the characteristic of being social outsiders.

They play no part in ruling the City nor is its history made by them, nor, even, are they romantic rebels against its injustices; . . . they are not citizens or they are the City's passive victims."[4]

With these "passive victims" of society's machinery Wright identifies in *The Green Wall* and subsequent collections. Automatic compassion for such individuals has been recognized as a touchstone in Wright's work since Auden made his observations. There are, however, differing ways of articulating that compassion. Many poems employ the objective method characteristic of the academic poets, whereas in others tension emerges between the strategies for control of emotions and the desire to speak directly in the poet's personal voice.

Often the author takes an objective stance, in which his preference for the attitude of the outcast is the result of juxtaposition of images rather than direct statement. "A Gesture by a Lady with an Assumed Name," for instance, could, except for its subject matter and tone, have been written by Wilbur or any skilled craftsman among the academic poets. Its six iambic pentameter quatrains rhyme *a b a b*, and intricate structural devices dictate our emotional response to the woman of dubious reputation whose death is the literal subject of the poem. In each of the first three stanzas, the accent of the third foot of the first line falls on the dominant syllable of *clutter,* and this repetition gains impact as types of clutter contrast one with another. Letters clutter her desk; laundry clutters her floor; and "Lovers she left . . . clutter up the town" (*CP,* 36). An inventory of the clutter she left behind accounts for exactly half the poem; the remaining three stanzas raise questions about her lovers and her effect on them.

Even the title presents a subtle enigma characteristic of the academic poets. Her "gesture" is her death, hardly the most voluntary of signs unless it were a suicide, but Wright's main concern is her friends' and associates' responses to her gesture. Her anonymity is carefully guarded. Her "assumed" name may be an alias or an ironic reference to the vacuum left by her anonymity. She has no name for the poet or the reader. The other characters of the poem remain equally anonymous, and even the speaker, mentioned as "I" in the final stanza, has no specific identity.

Wright controls the reader's response by listing inappropriate reactions to her death by those who knew her. The maid burns her letters, presumably personal communications that could give her an authentic identity, but steals her necklace. Her clothes and ribbons are appropriated by prostitutes to hang on their "rachitic skeletons." Many of her lovers "Mourned in the chilly morgue"—not a funeral parlor where mourning normally takes place—"and went away" (*CP*, 36). Other lovers, husbands who want to keep their association secret, lurk around the apartment house to intercept any incriminating evidence. This plunder and self-interest reinforce her anonymity and our sympathy for her.

In the last three stanzas, Wright questions the motives of the lurking lovers, and by doing so he expands the theme to comment on the problem of lovelessness in the modern world. "What were they looking for?" the speaker asks. He cannot provide a definite answer, so the poem ends in ambivalence. Were they merely trying to concoct a show of grief, "The cold pretense / Of lamentation offered in a stew?" (*CP*, 36). Or were they primarily self-centered, anxious to recover evidence of their contact with her? This possibility is certainly reinforced by the last lines, "I saw the last offer a child a penny / To creep outside and see the cops were gone"(*CP*, 36). Not only does the mourner's role reduce to self-interest, but the mourner implicates a child in the deception and furtiveness that characterize the poem.

Perhaps, Wright implies, a less ignoble motive governs the lurking of some of the lovers:

> Or did they rise to weep for that unheard-
> Of love, whose misery cries and does not care
> Whether or not the madam hears a word
> Or skinny children watch the trodden stair?
> (*CP*, 36)

The speaker cannot be sure that such a motive exists in any of them, and that final gesture, offering the child money to spy on the police, shows that it is far from universal. There is a remote possibility that some lovers want to understand the mystery of a type of love that is not furtive, that is indifferent to the opinions of the world. If this is so, her gesture implies another meaning: the possibility of a love quite opposite to the tawdry marketing of its shadow that characterizes her profession. Yet if such a motive should prompt certain lovers, it must include a recognition that her love is born of "misery." In any case, the mourners would be weeping for the kind of love the lady represented, and not for the individual who embodied that rare kind of love.

"A Gesture by a Lady with an Assumed Name" is an impressive achievement. It communicates intense emotions about the failure to associate sexual with spiritual love in the modern world, but the strategy is to present that emotion through images and rhetorical questions. By contrast, "To a Fugitive" does not maintain such an objective posture. Less successful than "A Gesture," this poem adapts the Italian sonnet form, but does not exploit the structure of problem-resolution implicit in that form; Wright would later attempt this experiment with greater success in "Saint Judas" and "Reading a 1979 Inscription on Belli's Monument." In his dream, the poet empathizes with an escaped criminal and associates Maguire with nature in ways that do not convince: "I dreamed you rose / Out of the earth to lean on a young tree" (*CP,* 27). The metaphor of Maguire's escape as a resurrection does not persuade because Maguire is not really a personality. We do not know what he did, how or why he escaped. The tree, always a symbol in Wright's poetry for the vital and nurturing presence of nature, seems arbitrarily related to this fugitive.

After the poet effectively dramatizes the police surrounding Maguire, the imagery fails him. He openly takes the convict's part against authority: "Strip, run for it, break the last law, unfold, / Dart down the alley, race between the stars" (*CP,* 27). Because we do not know Maguire's original offense or the attitudes of the officers, this endorsement of Maguire's break and potential death in a suicidal shoot-out seems arbitrary and unconvincing. Wright would seldom make this kind of mistake in the future. He tries to do too much in a small space. The sonnet is a constraint, because Wright cannot give sufficient details to make his endorsement of Maguire the reader's own. Without such specification, the pursuit is little more than a cliche from popular film. To identify with an escaped convict simply because officers pursue him is sentimental.

In the early poems, Wright generally avoided sentimentality by disciplining his attitude through traditional forms and by investing the details with a significance that makes it possible for the reader to understand and share his compassion. This is true of "She Hid in the Trees from the Nurses" and "Mutterings Over the Crib of a Deaf Child." In the former, Wright uses iambic tetrameter stanzas with alternating rhymes to create sympathy for a young girl who refuses to answer the summons to return to a mental hospital. We may legitimately ask why compassion works so well here but fails in "To a Fugitive," despite the fact that both poems ask the reader to identify with a person at odds with authority. In "She Hid," the situation is spelled out clearly. All the inmates have spent a portion of the day outdoors, and several have responded to the beauty around them. All but the heroine have accepted their institutionalization, and the girl, from her vantage point, "sees the undressed shadows creep / Through half-illuminated minds / And chase the hare and flower to sleep" (*CP*, 19). Her perception is Wright's way of telling us that the other patients are being returned not only to the walls, but to the deadness, of the institution.

It does not matter whether she realizes this; what matters is that we as readers comprehend an impulse she may not be able to explain. To help us share her feelings, Wright's speaker asks, "Why must a lonely girl run mad / To gain the simple, pure delight / Of staying . . .?" (*CP*, 20). We logically sympathize with the girl's impulse to prolong her contact with nature and night, to put off as long as possible her return to the asylum. We can accept her contrast of the "simple, pure delight" of nature as opposed to the dryness and regimentation inside. Wright causes us to wonder what madness really is, when these healthy impulses force us into conflict with those whose job is to make us well.

A similar fusion of metrical control and objective situation enables Wright to communicate a lovely emotion in "Mutterings Over the Crib of a Deaf Child." This poem, with its intricate rhyme scheme, is a dialogue in which a speaker asks questions about how the child can compensate for his handicap, and the child's mother replies. The first two questions are practical: how will the child know when it is time to come home from school, or when it is time to get up in the morning? The mother is confident that others will help the boy and that his other senses will enable him to know what most of us perceive by hearing.

In the fifth stanza, the questions become more philosophical: "what will you do if his finger bleeds? / Or a bobwhite whistles invisibly / And flutes like an angel off in the shade?" (*CP*, 37). To explain pain even to a hearing child is difficult, because it involves something irrational. How much harder it would be to explain it to a child who cannot hear. And the question about the bobwhite gets at the heart of the issue of sense deprivation. The child's experience

of the bird must be incomplete because he can see it but not hear its
music. How then can he know the bird? The mother's response
blends resignation to the inevitable, devotion, and love:

> He will learn pain. And, as for the bird,
> It is always darkening when that comes out.
> I will putter as though I had not heard,
> And lift him into my arms and sing
> Whether he hears my song or not.
>
> (CP, 37)

The mother's song can resonate in ways the bird's cannot. The mother
knows that she cannot make the child's experience complete and that
she cannot protect him, or anyone else, from pain. What she can do
is share his incompleteness by pretending she does not hear the bird
and offer him instead her human song of unconditional love.

The emotional success of "Mutterings" depends on its dialogue
structure. The poet communicates the simple beauty of the mother's
hope through her own words. Similarly, "Sappho" makes us feel the
alienation of its lesbian speaker as Wright uses the dramatic monologue. This poem is much more freely formed than most in *The Green
Wall*, perhaps because the literary tradition behind the dramatic
monologue has allowed sufficient flexibility to represent the rhythm
of conversational speech. The compassion here is far more complex
than in "To a Fugitive." The speaker is not an occasion for pity because she has homosexual tendencies, but because she cannot rebel
against the mores of a society that condemns her preference. She recalls an event in which her dull life as a housewife was momentarily
brightened by an unexpected visit from a woman who stirred her
erotic feelings. When the woman became close, the husband of the
visitor came "to pluck her like an apple," and the affair ended there.

Although her secret has been exposed, the speaker cannot assume
the attitude of a defiant rebel. The only emotion she feels toward the
society that spurns her is bitterness: "And now it is said of me / That
my love is nothing because I have borne no children" (CP, 34). Although she is determined not to let society's attitudes rule her own
sexual orientation, she is unable to rebel against custom. The allusion
to the classical lesbian who defied the heterosexual majority lends an
exceptional irony to this poem. Wright's Sappho will not create art
or celebrate lesbian love; she will privately and painfully cherish her

singular experience, while on the surface maintaining as much of the appearance of conformity as possible:

> I keep the house and say no words. . . .
> I will not douse that flame,
> That searing flower; I will burn in it.
> I will not banish love to empty rain.
>
> *(CP, 35)*

The speaker associates rain with love rather than sexual fertility, and in this stanza Wright uses paradox to suggest that, for a woman like his speaker, sex merely for reproduction is "empty."

A significant number of poems in *The Green Wall* employ allusion in the manner of the modern poets. Much of the impact of "Sappho" depends on an allusion to classical literature. "Erinna to Sappho" alludes to two ancient poetesses, rumored to have lived at the same time, and "Come Forth" retells the Lazarus story. "The Angel" is a dramatic monologue in which the angel who rolled away the stone before Christ's tomb meditates on the charms and limitations of being merely human. Despite his awareness of the limitations of human beings, the angel has his epiphany when he sees a young girl wash her hair. His entire perspective changes: "I stood there, sick to love her, sick of sky" *(CP, 38)*. Now the angel cannot be at peace in heaven, because he shares the desires of mortal men. Yet, because he is an angel, he cannot assume human form. The only benefit the angel derives, and it is enough, is an understanding of why Christ would die for the human race. He understands, through the sexual urge he felt, the spiritual love that led Christ to the tomb.

Many of the finest poems in *The Green Wall* present an intensely personal experience and emotion with the objectivity perfected by the academic poets. In poems like "The Horse" and "A Fit Against the Country" tensions develop between the urge to comment directly and the desire to exert formal control. In most of these, we hear a unique tone; aligned with the New England pastoral tradition, Wright, like Frost, balances his love of nature with a distinctly antipastoral feeling. Nature is the source of beauty and nurture, but it is also a source of anxiety because it frustrates our aspirations for unity with our environment. In "Lament for My Brother on a Hayrake," the harvest machine becomes a symbol for the harvester of souls, death itself, something that "Strips the revolving earth of more than grass" *(CP, 18)*.

Another poem about his brother, "To a Defeated Savior," ranks among Wright's best poems. The poet has said that this work was inspired by an event that happened when he and his brother were young. The poem itself, however, minimizes the autobiographical element. The persona, bearing no relation to the poet except for these external facts, enters into full empathy with the anonymous savior who failed. The issue is not the failure to save a drowning swimmer, but the lasting consequences of that failure. The speaker recalls that the youth can never look directly at that spot in the river. He also recognizes in occasional, unguarded facial expressions a reversion to the terrible scene at the river. The young man can engage in ordinary activities, but at those moments when his defenses are down, he is transported to the moment of his failure, to the "muddy banks and sliding shoals / You and the drowned kid tumble in" (CP, 20).

If the speaker shares the guilt of the defeated savior, Wright demands that we too participate in this universal failure. The savior was defeated not by the force of the river, but by a failure of nerve:

> You would have raised him, flesh and soul,
> Had you been strong enough to dare;
> You would have lifted him to breathe,
> Believing your good hands would keep
> His body clear of your own death:
> This dream, this drowning in your sleep.
>
> (CP, 21)

This youth had a unique opportunity to reach out, to risk his own life for the sake of a fellow human being, but he was not up to the challenge. His failure haunts him, and we and the speaker participate in reliving his inability to measure up to his moment of destiny.

This defeat represents the failure of all people at all times to reach out effectively to help one another: "The circling tow, the shadowy pool / Shift underneath us everywhere" (CP, 21). With this single stroke, Wright expands his situation to the universal. The undertow that drowned the swimmer becomes a synecdoche for the forces that threaten all humanity, so the savior's defeat, the inability to summon courage equal to the occasion, is everyone's failure. The speaker has compassion for the savior, because all human beings must share his guilt. Still, Wright does not excuse his failure. The poem demands that the savior, the speaker, and the reader come to terms with what might have been and, by extension, with the responsibility all human beings have toward one another.

Although a very different type of poem, "Arrangements with Earth for Three Dead Friends" also succeeds in bringing emotion under the control of form. The intricate rhyme pattern, *a b c d e e d c b a,* provides an order in this petition that the earth accommodate individuals by becoming for each a proper resting place. The poem celebrates the love we can have for the uniqueness of one another, even in death. The reader feels that these were very real people to Wright, but he adopts near-anonymity as his poetic voice. The speaker personifies earth as someone who can be appealed to reasonably and asks earth to reward each of his dead friends in a way that suits the personality the friend had in life.

The first two people for whom the speaker petitions are the kind for whom elegies have always been made. One is a joyful child, vital and so close to nature that he was "Wild as a beast but for the human laughter / That tumbled like a cider down his cheeks" (*CP,* 17). This lively child, like the girl in Ransom's "Bells for John Whiteside's Daughter," has vexingly returned to the source of his being, and the poet asks earth to provide him the same loving care his parents would if he had lived: "Receive his flesh and keep it cured of colds. / Button his coat and scarf his throat from snow" (*CP,* 17). The second, a singer or poet, will be "out of place" in a tomb because his vitality brought relief from despair and even happiness to all who knew him. The "bright earth" cannot give him anything, so the speaker asks earth to learn from this inhabitant: "Listen for music, earth, and human ways" (*CP,* 17). All we can ask of nature is that it be receptive to the full voice of the singer's humanity as representative of what is best in all of us.

In the appeal for the final friend, Wright brings an original twist to this elegy. She was not a pleasant person. She despaired that nature "broke for the sake of nothing human souls" (*CP,* 18). The earth should not be asked to protect her, like the child of stanza one, for "she was not inclined to beg of you / Relief from water falling or the storm" (*CP,* 18). Any attempt to comfort her would be an insult to her solitary and indifferent nature. She had integrity in her solitary ways, and Wright asks the "dark earth" to respect that stoic refusal to ask for nature's blessing: "Earth, hide your face from her where dark is warm. / She does not beg for anything, who knew / The change of tone, the human hope gone gray" (*CP,* 18). If she refused to seek the solace of nature or man, the only fitting tribute to her memory is to ask earth to respect the choices she made in life, and to let her alone.

Those tensions that have accumulated throughout *The Green Wall,* between the impulse to express personal feelings directly and the strategy of controlling those emotions by adopting the conventions of the academic poets, create the mood of the celebrated "Morning Hymn to a Dark Girl." This poem echoes Swift's "Description of the Morning" and Blake's "London" in its depiction of the City as a dreary and loveless place. The speaker presents a panoramic view of the despair of the citizens as they prepare for another grim day: the glum cop, the Negro driver, the asceptic girls, the windows of the rich, and the prostitute Betty, who prepares to sleep the day away.

Wright's speaker makes an arbitrary commitment to Betty that involves a personal, rather than a detached, voice: "I celebrate you, Betty, flank and breast" (*CP,* 31). The speaker celebrates not her sexuality, however, but her obliviousness to the despair of those around her. Wright compounds compassion with irony in a wonderful line that will echo in later poems: "Pity the rising dead who fear the dark" (*CP,* 31). Those who meet the world on its own terms are fated to despair, and Wright seems to praise Betty for her ability to dream on and evade that awful knowledge. If the logic of this praise is faulty— and it is—the intuition contains the potential for mature irony. Unlike Jenny, the prostitute and muse of later poems, Betty has, by refusing to accept the concerns of most of us, avoided for the moment the despair that may be the cultural legacy of modern mankind.

The poems collected in *The Green Wall,* while they do not bear the mark of the mature Wright, are impressive on the whole. Several offer permanent satisfaction to the careful reader. Quite a few reward continued reading with new insights and delights. If they are apprentice work, they are surely the work of a very precocious apprentice.

Saint Judas

Coming into print only two years after *The Green Wall, Saint Judas* seems on the surface to continue the formal restraint of the initial book. The basic line remains iambic, and rhyme continues, although less frequently, to unify the stanzas. Traditional forms like the sonnet and the dramatic monologue persist, and the stance is often objective. Yet the tensions between traditional and organic form felt in the earlier collection take on new intensity.

Always eager to unify a volume of poems, Wright has said that the composition of these helped him come to terms with personal anguish. He makes the reader aware of an intended unity by dividing the collection into three distinct parts. The first unit, eighteen poems about time and mutability, is called "The Lunar Changes." This group is followed by "A Sequence of Love Poems," prefaced by an epigraph from *King Lear:* "Thou know'st, the first time that we smell the air / We wawl and cry" (4.4.181–182). This is a curious introduction to eight love poems, but they deal with the loss and the frustrations to which we can become liable when we fall in love, rather than with love's joys. Many treat the death of a beloved and the tone is often anger the speaker feels because of some slight or disappointment during that person's life.

At the heart of *Saint Judas* are concerns like alienation, the love-hate relationship we all feel toward death, the inability to form a perfect union with others or with nature, the futility of trying to escape the past, and, of course, compassion for the unwanted and misunderstood of our society. In this collection, both poet and reader must come to terms with the humanity we share with the outcast by daring to reexamine our most fundamental beliefs about the self and the culture. We are forced to examine the premise that "guilt and innocence do not so much trade places as *homogenize,* . . . until the reader is forced to reconsider his own attitudes towards success and failure, praise and blame, tenderness and violence."[5]

Another theme that emerges in this book accounts for some of the restless growth that marked Wright's artistic life. Frequently, Wright questions the vocation of the poet. He does not automatically assume that poetry is a higher form of cognition; he risks examining the premise that poetry may be a way of escaping reality by creating an alternative to the grim truths we must learn to face. In that all poets have a vested interest in the superiority of poetry over more common forms of experience, this is a daring theme. The most extreme questioning appears in "At the Executed Murderer's Grave," in which Wright accuses himself of self-interest in transforming human agony into art: "I croon my tears at fifty cents per line" and "those giggling muckers who / Saddled my nightmares thirty years go / Can do without my widely printed sighing / Over their pains with paid sincerity" (*CP,* 83). In this version of the question, Wright implies that poets may sometimes exploit the suffering of others for their own artistic or merely material gain.

A less vehement discussion of the poet's role occurs in "The Moral-

ity of Poetry." Addressed to fellow poet Gerald Enscoe, this joins a
distinguished tradition of American seaside meditations on the function of the imagination. Obvious literary antecedents include Whitman's "Out of the Cradle Endlessly Rocking" and Stevens's "The Idea
of Order at Key West." Like Whitman and Stevens, Wright finds
that the origin of poetry is the cultivation of a disciplined imagination that responds to, but is not intimidated by, the raw material of
experience. For all three, the sea is a metaphor for the unchecked
power of nature. It is inscrutable and powerful, and if we cannot
bring our imagination to contain it, we risk being overwhelmed by
it. Like both predecessors, Wright employs a discursive structure to
meditate on the possible relationships between the individual and his
environment.

In the first stage of his argument, Wright weighs Enscoe's images
against the "roaring elegies to birds" he perceives while he observes
the sea. Using personification liberally to give artistic life to nature,
he sees in the motions of the sea a poem that is sufficient in itself.
Against this poem of nature, he contemplates the art of "your human
voice, / Flinging the poem forward into sound" (*CP*, 60). Human
imagery is mere artifice compared with the natural rhythms of the
sea. Yet the sea's natural poem has a disturbing element, because
while it composes "Slow celebration," it also casts up reminders of
our weakness in the face of its gigantic strength. When Wright mentions the flotsam and jetsam thrown up by the sea, his meditation
becomes a pessimistic contemplation of the brute force of the ocean.

Now thinking of the sea as "Sheer outrage hammering itself to
death" (*CP*, 60), Wright considers the gulls that flock by the hun-
dreds over it. These cannot console him, for the hundred "decline to
nothingness," and despair at ever bringing the mighty sea to imaginative synthesis reaches its most intense point. At precisely this moment, the speaker notes a single gull that "Shadows a depth in heaven
for the eye" (*CP*, 60). This leads the poet to the first major shift of
meaning in his discussion of aesthetics. He realizes the necessity of a
purely human vision to explain the kind of illumination the sight of
the lonely gull has brought him: "A single human word for love of
air / Gathers the tangled discords up to song. / Summon the rare
word for the rare desire" (*CP*, 60). Echoing Stevens's main theme,
Wright acknowledges the need for an ordering human voice to bring
perspective to the raw poem of the natural world.

If the rare word is to be summoned, there must be rules by which to organize it. Upon discovering that the rare word "thrives on hunger," or our awareness of a need to connect our experiences with nature through imagination, Wright creates a cluster of metaphors comparing artistic composition with the human body in order to establish classical rules for poetry. If the bones are spare and the muscles lean, the poem will be strong enough to clarify the chaos of nature. Often in interviews, Wright mentioned his debt to Horace, and in "Prayer to the Good Poet" he addresses Horace as his literary father. In "The Morality," the young poet lays down rules for poetry that reflect Horace's maxim, "prune your verses": "Before you let a single word escape / Starve it in darkness" (*CP,* 61). In "Epistle to the Pisos," Horace advised young poets to put away their verses for nine years before submitting them for publication. Wright clearly has something similar in mind when he tells Enscoe to "starve" his words in darkness and to prune them to terse, muscular form.

In this section, it seems that "The Morality" is anything but critical of the poet's art. By inferring a need for classical decorum, Wright endorses craft in poetry. Yet the poem undergoes a third shift in the final verse paragraph, and with that shift Wright again calls into question the artistic process.[6] Moving from the spirit of Stevens, seeking intellectual synthesis of the chaotic facts of experience, toward that of Whitman, seeking immersion in the flow of experience, Wright acknowledges the futility of ever composing rules adequate to construct poetry that represents the whole of our experience. The overt purpose of the meditation, to build rules by which poets can write, has proved a failure: "So through my cold lucidity of heart / I thought to send you careful rules for song" (*CP,* 61). Such rules would depend on a selective interpretation of experience. Wright is "ensnared" by the complexity of his perceptions, and he knows he cannot create rules sufficient to the task of representing: "I let all measures die. My voice is gone, / My words to you unfinished" (*CP,* 61). Honest contemplation of the data of experience "Flaunt[s] to nothingness the rules I made" (*CP,* 61).

Although the desire to reduce human experience to rules for composition has led to a dead end, the poem is not a record of failure. Wright has not abandoned the quest; he has simply learned that he must redefine his goal. "The Morality" ends on a note of ecstatic joy as the poet sends "you shoreward echoes of my voice" (*CP,* 61). At the beginning, poems were sent out over the sea, but now the voice of the poet merges with that of the sea, to speak not with the voice

of art, but with that of nature. All our rules can never bring us into
a position from which we can interpret nature. We must merge with
its imperfect and chaotic process, and take the risk Whitman did, to
speak without masks about the portions of the process we can understand. In a slightly later prose study of Whitman, Wright praised the
bard's "delicacy" and artistic courage in ways that are relevant to this
poem. He calls Whitman a model for contemporary poets because of
"the nobility of his courage," both aesthetic and moral, a courage embodied in his "powers of restraint, clarity, and wholeness, all of
which taken together embody that deep spiritual inwardness, that fertile strength, which I take to be the most beautiful power of Whitman's poetry, and the most readily available to the poetry, even the
civilization, of our own moment in American history."[7] The "Morality" of poetry, then, is to speak the truth and to hazard immersion
in the imperfectly understood processes of nature.

The literal subjects of *Saint Judas* are death and change. Many
poems are elegiac, but the strategies for dealing with these issues dif-
fer in ways that anticipate the revision of style Wright would soon
undertake. In some, the elegiac mood is communicated from the perspective of an uninvolved narrator, as in "Paul," a psychological study
of spiritual defeat. Paul's inability to rage at his wife's dying is communicated to us primarily by the imagery, and the poet builds compassion for men like Paul by means of contrasts: "She was lovely, she
was dead. / Some sparrows chirruped on a tree / Outside, and then
they flew away" (*CP,* 50). The reader is not asked to accept any specific judgment of Paul's reaction, but is rather moved to formulate
his own response by considering the details Wright provides.

Several other poems use traditional forms to create distance between the poet and his material. Dialogue between an interrogator
and the primary speaker objectifies "What the Earth Asked Me" in a
manner similar to Hardy's "The Sisters." "Complaint," like "Saint
Judas," uses the dramatic monologue to communicate ambiguity.
The exact emotion the speaker feels for his dead wife is not clear, and
this is the principal point of the poem. He seems to mean what he
says when he calls her "my moon or more" at the end of the first and
last lines. Yet when he lists her accomplishments, he views her as a
worker, not a whole person. She kept house, took care of domestic
animals, mended clothes, and "smacked the kids for leaping up like
beasts" (*CP,* 49). When he predicts a future without his life's companion, his language indicts his attitude: "What arm will sweep the

room, what hand will hold / New snow against the milk to keep it cold?" (*CP,* 49). The arm and hand, traditionally synecdoches for the involvement of the whole person, are reduced by this speaker to tools for menial chores. And the tasks become progressively undignified: who, now that she is gone, "will dump the garbage, feed the hogs, / And pitch the chickens' heads to hungry dogs?" (*CP,* 49). There is no hint that the speaker perceives the bitter irony of his answer, "Not my lost hag who dumbly bore such pain" (*CP,* 49). Wright's dramatic irony, wherein the speaker sees no contradiction between the insensitivity that allows him to call his wife a hag (because she conformed with his definition of a spouse's role) and the conventional language of the mourning lover, is the point of "Complaint." His love is not insincere; its self-serving sincerity is the most frightening thing about it.

In some of the best poems in *Saint Judas,* the objective stance favored by the academic poets comes into conflict with an individual urge to make a direct statement. The voice of these poems is lyric, inescapably the poet's own. The feeling in these works is so intense that it cannot be assigned to created personae, and the poet takes direct responsibility for the statement he is making. This does not mean that the emotion is less complex than in the more objective poems, but it does mean that the poet dares to address the reader directly about the content of the emotion. Comparable models include the kind of lyric we find in Wordsworth's Lucy poems or "Tintern Abbey," in many of Whitman's lyrics, in most of Frost's best work, or in the finest products of Yeats's mature period.

Wright's need to move beyond the self-contained, objective poem can be illustrated by considering "On Minding One's Own Business" and "Old Man Drunk," which share a tendency to combine the attitude of the autotelic poem with the need to lead the reader toward a proper interpretation of the events and imagery. Each begins, in Ransom's words, as "A Poem Nearly Anonymous," but each moves toward a direct personal interpretation of the details that make up the poem. Wright has not lost confidence in the power of his imagery. He has, however, gained the confidence in his vision to offer the reader something more than an impersonal image.

"Old Man Drunk" divides symmetrically between a portrait of the subject and the poet's commentary on that subject. Like the practice of the academic poets, the syntax of the title reveals something fundamental to the scene. The fact that he is not a "drunk old man" suggests that intoxication is incidental, not essential, to his nature. Readers familiar with Hemingway's "A Clean, Well-Lighted Place" will recognize in his drunkenness an attempt to maintain dignity in the face of despair. The old man has drunk himself into a stupor because his daughter "struck him in her grief / Across the face, hearing her lover dead" (*CP,* 51). He could not soothe her grief, because "An old man's fumbling lips are not defiled / By the sweet lies of love" (*CP,* 51). At the same time, he cannot deal with her hysterical anger, so he gets drunk.

Impressive as the portrait is, it gains meaning from the introduction of a speaker who is surely an extension of the poet. He "can say nothing" to comfort the old man, just as the old man could not comfort his daughter. He sees the old man as an Everyman figure, someone desperately holding onto a shred of dignity in the face of frustration and death. He sees his eventual fate, and everyone's, in this drunk's deliberate gaiety: "the many faces of old age / Flutter before me in the tavern haze" (*CP,* 52). Holding on to his dignity surely qualifies this man as one of the best faces of old age, a point Wright underscores with the brilliant simile, "Gay as a futile god who cannot die / Till daylight, when the barkeep says goodbye" (*CP,* 52). We respect the attempt the old man has made to deal with his situation, especially as we realize with him that any attempt to ward off despair is bound to be temporary. These emotions take on a rich relevance for us because within the poem Wright comes to terms with the humanity he shares with the unhappy old man.

Similarly, "On Minding One's Own Business" takes a seemingly objective stance toward the decision of the "Ignorant two" who row their boat away from an interesting shack on the shore to respect the privacy of whoever may inhabit it. Wright has explained that the poem modifies events that took place on a fishing trip with Richard Hugo.[8] Yet the autobiographical element is not crucial to the poem. Without this information, it communicates its meaning quite well. What distinguishes this poem is the pattern of generalization Wright develops to clarify his theme. We are not made aware of the decision-making process. The choice to mind their own business is almost accidental, but in the poem the fishermen learn the importance of their decision.

Wright generalizes the situation to include the lovers among all those who have reason to keep their privacy, and the apostrophe seeks

solitude not only for lovers, but for all the outcasts who make up
Wright's world:

> From prudes and muddying fools,
> Kind Aphrodite, spare
> All hunted criminals,
> Hoboes, and whip-poor-wills,
> And girls with rumpled hair,
> All, all of whom might hide
> Within that darkening shack,
> Lovers may live, and abide.
>
> *(CP,* 59)

By praying to the goddess of love, Wright petitions the reader to
grant privacy to all who need it. The poem persuades us because
Wright makes his generalizations explicit, yet allows the reader to
participate in drawing the appropriate inference.

In "At the Slackening of the Tide" and "All the Beautiful are
Blameless," the movement from contemplation of a scene of disaster
to personal evaluation of the implications of that catastrophe dictates
the central emotions. Both discuss a witnessed event, a woman who
laments over the drowning of her child and the recovery of the body
of a girl who drowned while swimming naked and drunk with "stupid harly-charlies." The imagery is vigorous, but each poem derives
its power from the poet's personal assessment of the scene he has been
forced to witness.

Wright's participation in the woman's grief in "At the Slackening
of the Tide" moves from despairing witness to the wish that he could
blot the memory from his mind, then to a reluctant acceptance of the
implications of the event. While the woman grieves hysterically and
the lifeguard suffers physical pain from his efforts to save the child,
Wright maintains the detachment of a reluctant observer who knows
the outcome will be dreadful, for when a dog discovers the body
washed back to shore, its bark "Announces everything I knew before"
(CP, 62). He considers the many human and animal wrecks now con-
signed to the ocean, and recalls Homer's descriptions of the sea.
When the catastrophe has been disclosed, Wright wishes to blot it
from his memory. Remembering his intention to spend a pleasant day
at the shore, he blurts out, "I would do anything to drag
myself / Out of this place" *(CP,* 62).

Scenes like this cannot be erased from the memory, and the poet must summon courage to face the awful implications of what he has witnessed. In his seaside prison, Wright daringly reverses the story of creation and alludes to Jonah's brooding and Pilate's denial of responsibility:

> Abstract with terror of the shell, I stared
> Over the waters where
> God brooded for the living all one day.
> Lonely for weeping, starved for a sound of mourning,
> I bowed by head, and heard the sea far off
> Washing its hands.
>
> (*CP, 63*)

Some of the beauty of these lines traces to the alternating of metrical and rhythmical lines, in which the cadence is determined by the rhythm of meditative thought. The emphasis on the isolation of the thinker, whose loneliness is paradoxically intensified by the contemplation of someone else's misfortune, adds intellectual and emotional weight to that beauty. His realization of nature's final indifference to human tragedies is the content of the poet's reluctant interpretation of the event, but the impact of this thought owes much to the daring comparison between the poet, who broods to understand tragedy, and God, whose brooding over the sea was the source of all life.

The situation in "All the Beautiful are Blameless" is similar, but the artistic strategy differs. Wright simply places his assessment of the girl's death in opposition to those of other observers. While "the starved, touristic crowd" would say that she got what she deserved for the foolish prank of swimming drunk, and while the "hired saviours" want only to recover the body and list her name, Wright sees her death as a recovery of the innocence she flaunted in her prank. He does not ignore the foolishness of her act or the ugliness of the corpse they drag to shore. He does insist that a transformation has taken place. As she died, she became part of nature, and therefore beyond praise or blame: "But the dead have no names, they lie so still, / All the beautiful are blameless now" (*CP, 64*). Wright does not exonerate the foolish girl, but he maintains his individual position, in the face of public opinion, that she has been transformed.

One of the most beautiful and disturbing of the love poems, "The Accusation," combines sympathy for the imperfect with graveyard meditation in an intensely personal way. There is no reason to doubt that the speaker is Wright himself, or that the poem treats a love affair that turned out poorly. The poet mourns his lost lover, but he more emphatically laments the fact that he was not allowed full participation in her life. She had an ugly birthmark, and the poet regrets that she hid this imperfection from him. What she never knew was that her flaw was a source of his love: "I loved your face because your face / Was broken" (*CP,* 71). Her unwillingness to let him look at the blemish was a refusal to share her uniqueness with him. No matter how intimate their relationship may have been, he cannot forgive her for not understanding that he loved her because of, not in spite of, this unique feature.

This poem is really a complaint. Denied access to her individual truth, the poet no longer remembers what his lover looked like; he recalls the "lovely emptiness" of many faces he has seen, but her distinctive beauty eludes him: "You had no right to turn your face / From me. Only the truth is kind" (*CP,* 72). Denied even the memory of her uniqueness, he blames her for his loss. He celebrates her imperfection as he speculates on a future without either her or an accurate memory of her:

> How can I ever love another?
> You had no right to banish me
> From that scarred truth of wretchedness,
> Your face, that I shall never see
> Again, though I search every place.
>   (*CP,* 72)

He can never love anyone else, but he celebrates her individuality as worthy of loyalty, despite the anger he feels because their relationship was incomplete. Even with God's power, to raise her from the dead, "I would bare to heaven your uncommon pain, / Your scar I had a right to hold, / To look on, for the pain was yours" (*CP,* 72).

Several fine poems in *Saint Judas* return Wright to scenes of his youth in Ohio, and in these, culminating in "At the Executed Murderer's Grave," the scenes from youth are vehicles for the poet's discovery of his identity. "An Offering for Mr. Bluehart" reflects on the poet's childhood pranks of stealing apples from the orchard of a neighborhood grouch. Wright makes ironic use of the Tom Sawyer motifs his chosen situation might imply, as he transforms this amus-

ing story of childhood mischief into an elegy that is at the same time
an attempt to exorcise personal guilt. Each stanza gathers to a peri-
odic reminder of the mutability of all things. In the first, the scene
of the boys' prank contains sparrows that "Denounced us from a broken bough." The mention of a broken bough transforms the tone
from the attitude of a prank to an elegiac tone that intensifies as the
sparrows "limp along the wind and die. / The apples are all eaten
now" (*CP, 50*).

Echoes of Eden are inherent in any story about orchards, apples,
trespassers, and guardians, and Wright emphasizes those contrasts by
associating the owner of this garden with the devil. Bluehart was a
"lean satanic owner" who lay in wait to catch his tormentors, and
"damned us to the laughing bone / And fired his gun across the
gray / Autumn where now his life is done" (*CP, 51*). This startling
juxtaposition of the old man's futile wrath, the actual threat against
the lives of the boys, their inability to take him seriously, and his
death creates a profound effect. His rage and their amusement were
part of a vast drama of decay, and the account of his violence blends
with that of his mortality. The mature Wright becomes retrospec-
tively aware of the seriousness of the trespass that was intended
merely as a prank: "We stole his riches all away" (*CP, 51*).

The final stanza contains Wright's "offering" for Bluehart:

> Sorry for him, or any man
> Who lost his labored wealth to thieves,
> Today I mourn him, as I can,
> By leaving in their golden leaves
> Some luscious apples overhead.
> Now may my abstinence restore
> Peace to the orchard and the dead.
> We shall not nag them anymore.
>
> (*CP, 51*)

The intended contrast between felt sorrow and an empty gesture of
abstinence is reinforced by the colloquial *nag* of the final line. Wright
knows that resisting the temptation to pick apples will not help his
dead adversary; at best it can appease the poet's own conscience. Yet
his recognition that this is all he can do suggests a discipline that will
enable him to respect others in the future. In this compelling explora-
tion of a trivial occasion for continuing human guilt, the poem speaks
eloquently to the need for all of us to be aware of the consequences

of our actions, for whatever we do to our fellow human beings will return to haunt us after it is too late to make retribution.

An Ohio memory also inspires "A Note Left in Jimmy Leonard's Shack," but unlike "Mr. Bluehart," this creates a current rather than retrospective account of an experience. Wright immerses the reader in the anxiety felt by a boy obligated to tell Jimmy, a notoriously violent town drunk, that Jimmy's brother has been pulled from the river. The child is trapped among many prohibitions; he will "get hell enough when I get home" for going to the shack; Jimmy has warned Minnegan not to go near the river, and the child fears that he will be blamed for Minnegan's disobedience; and Jimmy has warned the boys never to wake him when he is drunk. These anxieties combine to cause the boy to fear that Jimmy will punish the messenger for the content of the message, so he takes the easy way out. He writes the note that is the poem, and the final stanza combines rage and compassion in the coarse language of a frightened child:

> Beany went home, and I got sick and ran,
>   You old son of a bitch.
> You better hurry down to Minnegan;
> He's drunk or dying now, I don't know which,
> Rolled in the roots and garbage like a fish,
>   The poor old man.
>
> (CP, 54)

Until now, the reader has assumed that Minnegan is dead and has concentrated on the boy's fear of facing Jimmy. When we learn that Minnegan may still be alive, the passage of time becomes critical. Jimmy and the boy are locked in an unintentional conspiracy; Jimmy has terrified the child, and the boy has failed to wake him. While Jimmy sleeps, his brother may be dying, and the boy's failure to wake him may contribute to Minnegan's death. The child can do nothing to help him, without risking harm to himself, except to curse the drunken brother and pity the man whom no one else seems to care about.

As Wright returned to the Ohio of his youth and gradually abandoned the formal and objective procedures for writing poems to which he had been at best mildly loyal during the formative years, he was moving toward the style that would identify his voice in *The Branch Will Not Break*. The final stage of this movement can be seen in the finest poems from the final section of *Saint Judas*.

Murderers and Traitors: "Saint Judas" and "At the Executed Murderer's Grave"

The compassion for the outcast and criminal element in our society noted by Auden in his introduction to *The Green Wall* becomes a more subtle theme in *Saint Judas*. Readers are required to reevaluate, with Wright, their response to dramatically antisocial individuals in "The Part Nearest Home." The familiar theme takes on a new urgency, for what is at stake now is not merely our capacity for sympathy, but our understanding of our shared humanity. In "American Twilights, 1957" and "At the Executed Murderer's Grave," the voice is defiantly personal, and the process of defining the inference the poet intends us to share becomes the literal subject of the poems.

The title poem, which has occasioned as much critical controversy as anything Wright ever published, is a dramatic monologue and a magnificent farewell to a traditional form Wright had attempted in the first two books. The voice belongs to Judas, the betrayer of Christ and the most universally condemned man in Western literature. Formally, the poem is a Petrarchian sonnet. Wright came upon the idea of combining these forms as a technical experiment. He told an interviewer that he decided to write this poem after reflecting on the success of a similar experiment in Edwin Arlington Robinson's "How Annandale Went Out," an enigmatic account by a physician of the last moments of one of his patients. Always an admirer of Robinson, Wright decided to combine the same forms to capture a contradiction within the personality of history's greatest villain, and at the same time to challenge the reader's most basic attitudes toward Judas.[9]

Radical as this subject matter may be, there was a precedent in American poetry. In 1929, Jeffers published *Dear Judas*, a verse drama that attempted to explain the betrayal as motivated by Judas's excessive love both for Jesus and for mankind in general. Whereas Jeffers's drama is long and complicated, Wright's poem is brief and pointed. He does not treat motives behind the betrayal, but its immediate consequences. Saint Matthew (27.3–5) tells us that Judas committed suicide because he sold his master for silver, but Wright invents an episode while Judas is on the way to hang himself that provokes us to contemplate the residual decency in this, the worst of our fellow men.

The villain observes a gang of hoodlums beating up someone. This chance encounter with our human potential for cruelty enables Judas momentarily to forget the reprehensible crimes of his own immediate past: "I forgot / My name, my number, how my day began" (*CP*, 84). His human instinct forces him beyond both the narrowly personal identity formed by the betrayal and the intention to commit suicide, and he rescues the man.

Wright exploits the problem-solution structure inherent in the Petrarchian sonnet effectively. The sestet celebrates Judas's sainthood as the instinctive charity of a man who has decided to seal his own damnation by committing the unpardonable sin:

> Banished from heaven, I found this victim beaten,
> Stripped, kneed, and left to cry. Dropping my rope
> Aside, I ran, ignored the uniforms:
> Then I remembered bread my flesh had eaten,
> The kiss that ate my flesh. Flayed without hope,
> I held the man for nothing in my arms.
>
> (*CP*, 85)

These lines may be among the most moving in contemporary American poetry. Judas has absolutely nothing to gain from this moment of charity, and for this reason the moment affects us profoundly.

The words may move us, but there has been considerable disagreement on the discursive meaning of the lines. The key to the meaning is the phrase "for nothing." Its rich ambiguity has provoked contrary readings. John Ditsky associates the term with "bootless action," and therefore sees Judas's role as that of the alienated Christian existentialist "acting out a preordained role of whose personal pointlessness he alone is aware, that of the Good Samaritan." By contrast, Ralph J. Mills, Jr., focusing on the ambiguity of human behavior "between design and impulse," believes that the poem means that if one man can be at one moment desperate and treacherous, and at the next brave and selfless, we should all be more sparing in our judgment and more merciful toward our fellow men. Paul Lacey holds that Judas is not a case study in ethics or philosophy, but the "supreme riddle, the man who will do evil for pay, but good for nothing." Lacey quotes Wright on the intentions of the volume, intents that certainly apply to this poem: "I have tried to shape these poems, singly and as a group, to ask some moral questions: Exactly what *is* a good and humane action? And, even if one knows what such an action is, then exactly why should he perform it?"[10] This diversity of opinion indicates the richness of the poem and its capacity to speak to us. Certainly Wright asks us to reconsider our own interpretation of human nature, for in his fictional Judas he suggests that even the worst man in the least auspicious time is capable of an ethical action in and for itself, without an eye on rewards in either this world or the next.

Wright's method of developing a scene objectively, then generalizing its meaning and commenting directly on it, provides a sound technique for his poem to the rapist Caryl Chessman. "American Twilights, 1957" sees in Chessman's predicament a warning about the moral health of our nation. The first section is a crisp, detached portrait of the inside of a prison. The second indicates that Wright means his scene to be a warning about the spiritual condition of America: "Lie dark, beloved country, now" (*CP,* 80). A moral twilight for our nation, beloved as it and its principles may be, awaits if we citizens ignore our human bond with these prisoners.

The antidotes Wright proposes are to seek in the prisons the secret of our buried savage selves: "Seek him behind his bars, to crack / Out the dried kernel of his heart" (*CP,* 80). The outlaws have acted upon that buried impulse, and we must learn from them if we are to prevent our stupor—believing that we can contain the savage by building prisons—from allowing the twilight of 1957 to become total darkness. This is our intellectual salvation; spiritual salvation depends on our capacity to pray even for the most criminal of our kind: "God, God have pity on man apart" (*CP,* 80).

More even than Judas or Chessman or the many outcasts who populate *Saint Judas,* an unimportant cab driver from Bellaire, Ohio, tests the full capacity of Wright's, and our, sympathy. George Doty drove a girl out into the country, raped, then killed her. He was tried, convicted, and executed. Wright could not rid himself of Doty as an emblem for problems like capital punishment and the social impulse to protect ourselves by identifying certain people as evil and sequestering them. He had to try again and again to come to terms with Doty.

His first attempt appears in *The Green Wall.* "A Poem About George Doty in the Death House," although controlled by traditional forms, risks a simplistic identification with Doty as an object of wonder, the man who faces certain execution at a defined moment, "The simple, easy terror." Overstated empathy at the expense of even the victim, like "I mourn no soul but his, / Not even the bums who die, / Nor the homely girl whose cry / Crumbled his pleading kiss" (*CP,* 26), has provoked some not entirely unjustified objections from readers who object to easy sympathy for the criminal rather than the victim.

The compassion for Doty and not his victims may be difficult to excuse, but it is not hard to understand in relation to the theme. Wright sees Doty's crime as a brutish attempt to escape the loneliness that is our human condition:

> Caught between sky and earth,
> Poor stupid animal,
> Stripped naked to the wall,
> He saw the blundered birth
> Of daemons beyond sound.
> Sick of the dark, he rose
> For love, and now he goes
> Back to the broken ground.
>
> (*CP*, 26)

Wright does not excuse Doty so much as see in him a type for the man who cannot be satisfied with the alienation into which we are all born. Doty, not successfully constrained by the civilizing values of culture, acted brutally in response to a universal desire to overcome his fundamental alienation.

The long struggle to acknowledge his human ties with Doty was a watershed in the development of Wright's poetry. Before the revision of "At the Executed Murderer's Grave" prepared for *Saint Judas*, two versions were printed in *Botteghe Oscure* and *Poetry*. In both, Wright uses rhyme to articulate the need to recognize that element he must share with the killer, but in each the effect is bombastic. The *Poetry* version reads:

> Father and citizen,
> Myself, I killed this man:
> For the blind judges in my heart cried *Stone,*
> *Stone the murderer down!*
> So the blind murderer in my heart bowed down:
> I flung my stone, and now myself turn stone.

Despite the sincerity of this judgment of the culpability of any man in the fate of another, this version lacks the authority of the poem in *Saint Judas*. Wright told an interviewer that he had sent it to James Dickey because "it was a mess, full of mythological and biblical references and so on, very Victorian." He studied Dickey's comments carefully, and while returning by train from defending his Ph.D. dissertation, "rewrote it without looking at the previous version, from the beginning, and rewrote it as straight and direct and Robinsonian as I could make it," replaced the epigraph from Tate with one from Freud, and dedicated the final draft to Dickey.[11]

The poem in *Saint Judas* far surpasses the previous attempts precisely because it is structured as a meditation on brotherhood and human responsibility. In the seven sections, Wright moves through an astonishing variety of attitudes toward Doty. The pattern is from loathing and contempt for the killer to acceptance of their common humanity. In this acceptance, he is forced to consider the meaning of personal identity and integrity with the same honesty that would distinguish the volumes to come.

Wright begins with a declaration of personal identity that startles readers comfortable with the studied anonymity of much modern poetry:

> My name is James A. Wright, and I was born
> Twenty-five miles from this infected grave,
> In Martins Ferry, Ohio, where one slave
> To Hazel-Atlas Glass became my father.
> He tried to teach me kindness. I return
> Only in memory now, aloof, unhurried,
> To dead Ohio, where I might lie buried,
> Had I not run away before my time.
> Ohio caught George Doty.
>
> *(CP, 82)*

Only the most dedicated new critic would claim that "James A. Wright" is a persona invented by a poet named James Arlington Wright to serve the purposes of particular poem. These lines are a defiant attempt by a poet to speak in his own voice about the implications of any claim to personal identity. What, after all, does it mean to say one's name? Surely the saying of a name implies an understanding of the unique combination of experiences that makes up an individual personality. The elements of identity include place of birth, economic conditions, a loving father who tried to teach his son virtue, and a frightening antifather who, unlike the poet, was "caught" by Ohio.

Wright's first hypothesis is that what differentiates the man whose name is James A. Wright from the villain named Doty is escape. The "infected grave," later described as a "gash" that "festers," is symptomatic of the infectious death of spirit that takes place in Ohio, for "Dying's the best / Of all the arts men learn in a dead place" (*CP*, 82). Wright escaped the spiritual decay that motivated Doty's perverse claim for love as well as the retribution of a society that lives by the code of an eye for an eye: "And yet, nobody had to kill him either" (*CP*, 83). Becoming a poet and commentator on events, he seems almost safe from the death of the soul symbolized by "dead Ohio." Yet, as we saw in a previous section of this chapter, Wright distrusts any poet who "add[s] my easy grievance to the rest" (*CP*, 82).

No escape from Ohio was ever complete for Wright. Doty's crime and the vengeance of Belmont County haunt his memory, and he attempts to mitigate his guilt by feigning indifference: "Doty, if I confess I do not love you, / Will you let me alone?" (*CP*, 82). This artificial limit on human compassion evades the issue, for Wright knows that the real challenge is not to escape from or to excuse the actions of the killer, but to wrestle with the dread of recognizing that he shares humanity with the murderer and to establish a viable relationship between himself and the political entity that electrocuted Doty. This will require that Wright evaluate all claims on his compassion.

He seems to reject uncritical compassion for all outcasts when he says: "And no love's lost between me and the crying / Drunks of Bellaire, Ohio, where police / Kick at their kidneys till they die of drink. / Christ may restore them whole, for all of me" (*CP*, 83). Even this abdication of responsibility to God contains an ambiguity, for we may, indeed probably should, read the final line as saying that the poet's own wholeness depends on Christ's restoration of the outcasts. In any case, this attempt to differentiate between Doty and the other victims of society leads to the meditative climax of the poem: "I do not pity the dead, I pity the dying" (*CP*, 83).

The reference to Christ moves the poem from human imperfection to divine Justice, and Wright is able to resolve the dilemma of empathy with Doty while recognizing his brutality by contemplating the Last Judgment in the magnificent climax, when the "princes of the sea" descend

> to judge the earth
> And its dead, and we dead stand undefended everywhere,

> And my bodies—father and child and unskilled criminal—
> Ridiculously kneel to bare my scars
> My sneaking crimes, to god's unpitying stars.
>
> Staring politely, they will not mark my face
> From any murderer's, buried in this place.
> Why should they? We are nothing but a man.
>
>   (*CP,* 84)

If all of us, hardened criminals like Doty and meditative poets like Wright, are guilty of imperfections, how can we mere mortals presume to know what in the eyes of God will distinguish those who have acted on their worst impulses from those who have been able to control them? Perhaps on the Day of Judgment, we shall all have to acknowledge our shared humanity before God and affirm the human community in his presence. We are, after all, "nothing [more or less than] a man."

Wright was often challenged because of his compassion for the brutal Doty. In 1973, he told an audience about a letter he had received, and his response explains many of the themes we have discussed: "I told her that as far as I was concerned there was no doubt that Doty, as she had put it, had gotten 'exactly what he deserved.' I was not trying to defend or excuse him. What the poem tries to say is simply this: I pray to God that I don't get exactly what I deserve."[12] By considering the Last Judgment, Wright is able to resign himself to his community with Doty, as "killer, imbecile, and thief: / Dirt of my flesh, defeated, underground" (*CP,* 85). His recognition of Doty's evil blends with resignation to those bonds that unite poet and killer as participants in human nature.

"At the Executed Murderer's Grave" is not just a poem about compassion for one of society's enemies. It is a stern and powerful meditation on coming to terms with the nature we share with the very worst of our species. It is a major breakthrough in Wright's development as a poet, for the directness of statement and uncompromising emotional honesty his material forced upon him would become his true voice in *The Branch Will Not Break* and the succeeding collections.

Chapter Three
"The Kind of Poetry I Want": *The Branch Will Not Break*

Agreement is rare among literary critics, but *The Branch Will Not Break* has been consistently recognized as one of the most important collections of poetry published in America during its decade. With Kinnell's *Flower Herding on Mount Monadnock* and Bly's *Silence in the Snowy Fields,* this volume clarified one of the directions the new poetry would take, in direct reaction to the kind of academic poetry with which Kinnell and Wright had experimented in their early books.

Although the tensions already apparent in *Saint Judas* anticipated the new style of *The Branch Will Not Break,* a substantial change certainly took place between 1958 and 1964. What constitutes that change has been debated by the critics. Stepanchev exaggerates the shift by saying the new book "represents a drastic change in technique, subject matter, and tone," whereas Seay comes close to the mark when he says the real difference "was not a totally changed sensibility but a radically altered concept of what a poem should reveal about experience." Breslin offers the intriguing notion that with the new book, Wright had come to think of the poem, not as an autotelic entity, but as a "corridor" or "passageway into and beyond the physical world." Zweig emphasizes the example to other artists when he says that Wright's work took on a visionary quality that appealed to young poets as an alternative to the formal, elaborate rhetoric of Lowell and Wilbur, and James Dickey, writing for the cover of *Collected Poems,* observes that "Wright is one of the few authentic visionary poets writing today."[1]

A minor but revealing change in attitude is reflected by some of the titles in *The Branch Will Not Break* and *Shall We Gather at the River.* Wright displays a fondness for witty titles, often longer than the lines of text, like "As I Step Over a Puddle at the End of Winter, I Think of an Ancient Chinese Governor" and "Depressed by a Book of Bad Poetry, I Walk Toward an Unused Pasture and Invite the In-

sects to Join Me." These defy the reader's expectation for an epigram-
matic title and for the traditional well-made poem with which he had
increasingly struggled while writing *Saint Judas*.

Wright deliberately reduces his dependence on the iambic line and
end rhyme. Intensifying experiments he had undertaken in "A Note
Left in Jimmy Leonard's Shack," he attempts to capture the rhythms
of speech, with colloquialism, sudden shifts in meaning, and occasional crudities of language. Except for occasional poems like "Two
Horses Playing in the Orchard," he virtually ceases to use rhyme to
control the expression of emotion. Wright often referred to his movement away from these forms as an effort to cure himself of "glibness,"
which he regarded as the single most dangerous temptation in his
verse. He once said, "I suffer from glibness. I speak and write too
easily. . . . And that is why I have struggled to strip my poems
down." An earlier letter to Madeline DeFrees develops this idea more
fully, with specific application to the changes he was undertaking
while writing the poems in *The Branch Will Not Break:*

As for my own experiments, let me say only that they are at once more complex—and tentative—than they may seem. I realize that they are small and
fragmentary. . . .[M]y own poems are merely attempts to cure myself of
glibness. Glibness is the worst thing that can happen—and not only in the
writing of verse. Well, it was happening to me. So I started to fight it—I
did so by leaping outside of every technical trick I had learned.[2]

It should be observed that Wright does not see his shift in technique
as radical, even though he believed that he was evolving toward
greater authenticity in emotion and expression. He would find this
authenticity by exploring open forms.

Experimentation with open forms, as well as a more subtle use of
metaphor and imagery, can be seen in "Goodbye to the Poetry of Calcium." Both a new consciousness of how a poem should work and a
determination to fashion a vital relation with his environment form
the central concerns of this apostrophe to a muse he is leaving behind
him:

> Mother of roots, you have not seeded
> The tall ashes of loneliness
> For me. Therefore,
> Now I go.
>
> *(CP,* 111–12)

This muse is androgynously "mother of roots," "father of diamonds," "girl," "Tiller of waves," and "Mother of window sills and journeys." It is tempting to see in "roots" a pun on the literary mentors of Wright's other books as well as the origins in local scenes of many of his poems, but the critical point is that this muse has failed the poet. She has not given life to his waste land, and as he looks over his work to date, "The sight of my blind man makes me want to weep" (*CP*, 112). Dissatisfied with his poems while he was loyal to this muse, and unable to express concretely his relationship with the world around him, the poet feels despair: "Look: I am nothing. / I do not even have ashes to rub into my eyes" (*CP*, 112). His only recourse is to leave "the Poetry of Calcium," the hard, well-crafted artifacts of his early works, and to venture more daring forms.

By comparing "Goodbye to the Poetry of Calcium" with the *ars poetica* of *Saint Judas,* we can understand the crucial stylistic and structural difference between the first two books and the central volumes. In the tradition of Wordsworth, Frost, and Whitman, "The Morality of Poetry" was a meditative or discursive lyric. In such a poem, the poet contemplates a scene or event and guides the reader through a series of logical reflections about the implications of the subject, until a reasonable conclusion is reached by both poet and reader. "Calcium," like many poems in *The Branch Will Not Break,* is a lyric, but a new kind of lyric. The authenticity of the thought or emotion derives not from discursive reasoning, but from imagery. The reader participates with the poet in discovering, through intuitive understanding of the content of the images, an association between the image and the idea or emotion central to the poem. This process builds on the concept of the deep image examined in the first chapter, but it is not limited by the arbitrariness often associated with the deep image school of writing.

Several attempts have been made to label this process. Moran and Lensing coined the "emotive imagination" to describe the process of leading the reader "to understanding through feelings rather than through cluttered and structured intellectuality"; Jannsens calls the term into question because he finds in Wright's poems "a toughness of logical coherence" usually absent in the work of advocates of the new subjectivity. Breslin prefers "imagistic lyric," in which the "images themselves, while they partly refer to a literal scene, also enact metaphoric transformations" and "suggestions of invisible, magical realities beyond the physical world." Williamson suggests that the purpose of such poetry is to force "language to transcend itself."[3] Whatever term we use to describe the practice—perhaps "imagistic" or associative lyric will serve—it enabled Wright to fuse elements of the deep image with the profoundly personal voice he had been developing in a style that is spare, conversational, and rhetorical.

Undoubtedly, many causes can be found for the choices Wright made to take this direction in his art. Among these would be his association with Bly, which led him to think through the possibilities of surrealism and the deep image poetics Bly was working out at the time. Bly also encouraged him to translate the works of Spanish and Latin American writers, and this reinforced the directions Bly was taking. Perhaps the strongest single impetus for this particular direction came from his own decision to reread, then to translate, poems by Georg Trakl.

Wright had discovered Trakl (1887–1914) while he was on a Fulbright in Austria in 1952–53. In 1961, he and Bly brought out a translation, *Twenty Poems of Georg Trakl,* through Bly's Sixties Press. In a later tribute, "Echo for the Promise of Georg Trakl's Life," Wright called him "Father of my sound, / My poor son" (*CP,* 180), and thereby linked him with Horace among the poets he acknowledged as literary ancestors. Dying too early to be associated with the surrealists whom Bly encouraged Wright to emulate, Trakl achieved a personal, imagistic style similar to the one Wright would develop. The Austrian employed irrational materials in an effort to come to coherence, and this is exactly what Wright does in his best poems. Images may seem to be linked in an irrational manner, but there is usually a coherence behind the link if we as readers are patient and perceptive enough to discover it.

Wright frequently acknowledged Trakl's influence on him. His introduction to *Twenty Poems* emphasizes the organic unity within these poems: "We are used to reading poems whose rules of traditional construction we can memorize and quickly apply. Trakl's poems, on the other hand, though they are shaped with the most beautiful delicacy and care, are moulded from within. He did not write according to any 'rules of construction,' traditional or otherwise, but rather waited patiently and silently for the worlds of his poems to reveal their own natural laws." Fifteen years later, he explained Trakl's appeal in language that applies directly to *The Branch Will Not Break,* saying that he "writes in parallelisms, only he leaves out the intermediary, rationalistic explanations of the relation between one image and another." He admitted that "Trakl has had as much influence on me as anybody else has had." In fact, one critic believes that Trakl's influence "provided Wright with a new form for struggling against his taste for fancy writing" by showing him ways to use images to refer directly to intense emotions, and thus to create the emotions in the reader rather than to tell the reader what emotions are appropriate.[4]

We may see how valuable an ally Wright found in the Austrian by examining one of Wright's translations. "De Profundis," readily available in *Collected Poems,* develops many structures Wright was already exploring. Each of the diverse images for the evening that will be personified as "melancholy" captures a somber auditory or visual sense of a generalized evening, an "it." That unspecific sense is immediately modified as the poet describes two figures on the canvas. Each has a surreal quality. The "soft orphan" gathering corn has eyes that "graze" the landscape, and the explanation for her grazing eyes takes us into the realm of religious myth: "her womb awaits the heavenly bridegroom" (*CP,* 97). A parallel portrait is a shepherd, who, at an indeterminate time, "found the sweet body / Decayed in a bush of thorns" (*CP,* 98). Readers who expect narrative sequence may assume that the body is that of the orphan, but there is no proof of this in the poem. The portraits may be either sequential or simultaneous. If the former, we cannot know how much time separates the two. What they have in common is conceptual, not narrative. The mention of heavenly, shepherd, and thorns naturally suggests Christian emblems, but we are dealing with suggestion, not allegory. The shepherd is not Christ, and the thorns are bushes, not crowns. The two images link finally by being portraits of disappointed religious expectations.

That religious tone introduces a personal, subjective speaker who is alineated, God-like, and a deep imagist:

> I am a shadow far from darkening villages.
> I drank the silence of God
> Out of the stream in the trees.
>
> (*CP,* 98)

These mixed communions with nature are perfect for this poem about estrangement, and the speaker is helpless to intervene in the scene before him because at night, "I found myself in a pasture, / Covered with rubbish and the dust of stars" (*CP,* 98). If we do not see how one can be both submerged in trash and miracle, our patient intuitions will tell us that we must be both. We are human, and that means, for Trakl and Wright, that we have the radiance of heaven and the legacy of the environmental irresponsibility of our kind. This poem, like many of Trakl's Wright translated, suggests that the Virgil who guided Wright between the perils of irrationally deep imagery and extreme confessionalism was Georg Trakl.

The poems in *The Branch* and subsequent volumes treat directly a struggle to discover and comprehend the identity of the subjective, personal self of the poet. This concern had been the animating force of the final version of "At the Executed Murderer's Grave," where Wright announced his name to open his meditation on his community with Doty. In the present collection, he refers directly to his own pain, or more rarely his sudden joys, in almost every poem. Certainly Wright was encouraged to make his subjective states the locus of his poems by the prominence of confessional poetry.

He is not, however, a confessional poet any more than he is a deep image poet. Like the confessional writers, he attaches great importance to his private states of feeling, and like many of them he uses images that resonate with essentially private associations. His orientation, like that of the deep image poets, is more Jungian than Freudian. He is not interested in his neurosis, or his individual psychological deviations from the norm, as primary material for his poems. Whereas Plath makes grim jokes about her suicidal tendencies in "Lady Lazarus" and exhibits compulsively her unresolved feelings about her father in "Daddy," or Lowell announces his loathing of self and family tradition throughout *Life Studies,* Wright treats his personal moods as representing the universal difficulty of forming a meaningful bond with nature or human society. His images, rather than making statements about his private emotional difficulties, approximate the universality of the archetype.

This fundamental difference between Wright and the confessional poets can be illustrated by studying the fine, and frequently discussed, "Lying in a Hammock at William Duffy's Farm in Pine Island, Minnesota." From its witty title to its last shocking line, this has been an occasion for controversy about the central poetic strategies of *The Branch Will Not Break.*[5] The final line, which Williamson identifies as a translation of *"J'ai perdu ma vie"* from Rimbaud's "Song of the Highest Tower," sounds very much like the climactic lines of Lowell's "Skunk Hour": "My mind's not right" and "I myself am hell." The effect, however, is substantially different. Unlike Lowell,

Wright does not confess his immersion in the neurosis of society, but dramatically recognizes a remediable condition. If he could attain the harmony of the natural things he sees from the perspective of the hammock, he would presumably cease to waste his life.

This possibility is suggested by the elaborate organization of the poem. Although Stitt may overstate the case by saying the poem has the effect of a sonnet, a calculated order does prepare the reader for the sudden intrusion of the poet's own subjective and radical emotion. Four separate perceptions organize the poem into units of meaning, and all derive intensity from the shock of the final line, "I have wasted my life." The first is visual, but by no means objective. A "bronze butterfly" sleeps on a tree trunk above the reclining poet, "Blowing like a leaf in green shadow." The butterfly is static—sleep and shadow connote mortality—but the portrait emphasizes gentle motion, in complete harmony with the setting. "Bronze" suggests color, but it also hints at metamorphosis, for bronze is a material for statues, permanent human devices to arrest change. If these hints are caught by the reader, the butterfly is at once paradoxically static and dynamic, permanent and temporal.

The second image is auditory and again subjective. Cowbells "follow one another / Into the distances of the afternoon" (*CP,* 114). The bells, devices to locate cattle, are also synecdoches for the motion of the cows. For Wright, they measure distances, and in turn suggest movement toward death. The third image is visual and even more subjective than the previous two. The poet observes that the "droppings of last year's horses / Blaze up into golden stones" (*CP,* 114). The reader is startled by this transformation. Because of the effect of the sunlight on the perceiver, the waste has taken on the radiance of precious metal. The verb *blaze* connotes a useful alteration of matter, like burning. This emphasis on the mind's ability to imagine transformations should not obscure the fact that the droppings are of "last year's" horses, a syntactic reminder of the mutability of living things, while the human mind searches for permanence.

In the final image, "A chicken hawk floats over, looking for home" (*CP,* 114). The poet sees this while "evening darkens," so it is a perception connected with the end of day. The bird rides effortlessly on the wind, like the butterfly in the first image. By contrast with the butterfly's harmony in its environment, the hawk is "looking for home." It too is a displaced creature, and with the ominous elements of the previous three images, the quest for home may also associate with death. The poem hints that the hawk may find its temporal home, in stark contrast with human beings who must continue to seek.

The final line is not, then, a confession, but a discovery. It is the kind of realization that can occur when we meditate freely on the mutability of all things and the unique human property of anticipating our mortality. If the line exaggerates, it hyperbolically communicates that in such moments of recognition, whatever we have done in the small time we have will not be enough. Wright's translation of Hesse's *Wandering* provides a useful gloss for the effect of "Lying in a Hammock": "I have wasted half my life trying to live his life. . . . I increased the world's guilt and anguish, by doing violence to myself, by not daring to walk toward my own salvation."[6]

"Daring to walk toward my own salvation" expresses a central theme of *The Branch Will Not Break*. Whereas Wright organized *Saint Judas* by dividing the book into three sections, he uses a more subtle device to direct this collection. Taken as a whole, the book reads as a quest to discover a wholesome relation between the alienated poet and his environment. Stitt identifies the goal of the quest as simple happiness, and his synopsis of the quest, while somewhat more rigidly ordered than the actual sequence of the poems, provides useful guidance: "In his search for happiness, for comfort, for consolation, and for sustenance, the poet turns from the city to the country, from society to nature, from human beings to animals, and from a fear of the finality of death to a trust in immortality."[7] Although the book is not quite that symmetrical, the movement of the collection is to discover strategies for dealing with alienation. The principal sources of alienation to be overcome are society and politics, and the nature that offers us both hope and despair.

The Challenge of Politics and Society

The sympathy with outcasts in the first two volumes had really been a mild protest against political repression and complacency, and by the time Wright finished "At the Executed Murderer's Grave" he had come to recognize how much the inflexibility of political institutions contributes to the alienation of individuals. With the increasing confidence that enabled him to tackle new forms and to speak with a more personal voice in *The Branch*, the poet turned his attention frequently to the question of living with others in groups—politics. His poems on politics usually despair of remedies for the conditions that such institutions impose on individuals, so their function is diagnostic rather than therapeutic.

The first poem in the collection, "As I Step Over a Puddle at the End of Winter, I Think of an Ancient Chinese Governor," despite its witty title, associates the plight of the ninth century poet-statesman Po Chu-i, who wrote the epigraph Wright uses but is saluted as merely a "balding old politician," with the circumstances of the contemporary poet in middle America. Wright guesses at the anxiety with which Po set out toward "some political job or other," but only speculates on Po's fate: "You made it, I guess, / By dark" (*CP*, 111). What organizes the poem is not the narrative about Po, but an association of the uncertainty of his fate with that of the modern, isolated poet who cannot find a reliable set of public values in his society:

> Where is the sea, that once solved the whole loneliness
> Of the Midwest? Where is Minneapolis? I can see nothing
> But the great terrible oak tree darkening with winter.
> Did you find the city of isolated men beyond the mountains?
> Or have you been holding the end of a frayed rope
> For a thousand years?
>
> (*CP*, 111)

Po's fate and Wright's circumstance pose an implicit question of the relation of politics and personal destiny, as well as estrangement from nature's healing potential. In the mystery surrounding Po's destiny, Wright sees a paradigm for the uncertainty of his personal fate and that of modern Americans in a society that provides no meaningful public values. In our search for functional values, we may, like the Chinese poet-politician, be holding the end of a frayed rope.

Rituals that may take the place of authentic public values are the subject of the splendid "Autumn Begins in Martins Ferry, Ohio." Unlike many poems in the collection, the poet's identity is not in question here. He is a detached observer who, while he watches a football game in his high school football stadium (Martins Ferry High School was dedicated in 1924 as the Charles R. Shreve School), imagines the circumstances of many of the players' parents:

> I think of Polacks nursing long beers in Tiltonsville,
> And gray faces of Negroes in the blast furnace at Benwood,
> And the ruptured night watchman of Wheeling Steel,
> Dreaming of heroes.
>
> (*CP*, 113)

Frustration unites these citizens of the Ohio valley. They work hard
at unrewarding jobs, then get drunk in local bars. The aspirations
they have left are only dreams, and an American equivalent for the
hero is the athlete. Because their real lives are so empty in comparison
with their ability to dream, "All the proud fathers are ashamed to go
home." They are certainly not the heroes, even to their families, they
have the capacity to dream about, and their failure may render them
sexually impotent, for their wives are "Dying for love." The wives,
and by extension entire families, are victims of the emptiness the husbands feel.

This extension is fully realized in the final stanza:

> Therefore,
> Their sons grow suicidally beautiful
> At the beginning of October,
> And gallop terribly against each other's bodies.
>
> (*CP,* 113)

Open form serves Wright well here. The isolation of "therefore" introduces a causal sequence, one that indicts and at the same time celebrates modern institutional life. The youths train and sacrifice to live
out the frustrated dreams of their fathers, and the ritual of harvest is
replaced by a gladitorial contest. Their athletic skills and developed
bodies are sources of beauty, but the controlled violence on the field
is suicidal. The pointlessness and chaos of the contest are emphasized
by a reverse personification, in which men gallop in a harmful frenzy,
like stampeding beasts. Community rituals have degenerated to epi-
sodes of institutionalized violence in which the sons are victims of
their fathers' aspirations, and the implication is that they will sire
sons who will in turn sacrifice for them. In this powerful social commentary, which may suggest destructive effects of American industrial capitalism and our puritan heritage,[8] Wright does not lose sight
of the beauty of the boys' athletic skill or of their willingness to fill
the void in their fathers' wretched lives.

The political poems at the center of the collection employ the
poet's personal voice even less directly than "Autumn Begins." "In
Memory of a Spanish Poet," "The Undermining of the Defense Economy," and "Eisenhower's Visit to Franco, 1959" depend entirely on
contrasts and imagery for their social comments. In the first, the poet
Miguel Hernandez, a political prisoner, continues to write and his

words becomes seeds, "A greeting to my country" (*CP*, 123). The second, with a title reminiscent of many of Bly's, treats the dehumanizing effects of an economy based on military spending in which beautiful girls "can't be sold" and little boys awakening with new sexual energy are "Delicate little boxes of dust." The ripening pumpkin in a field is "yellow as the face / Of a discharged general" (*CP*, 123). All natural things have been contaminated by the false and destructive basis for our economy.

Wright's impersonal stance, rare as it is in *The Branch Will Not Break,* creates a scathing indictment of institutions as enemies of human harmony with nature in "Eisenhower's Visit to Franco, 1959," which appealed to Bly because "Everything is said with images. The poem is obviously one of the best political poems written in the U.S. for several years, and it becomes so without the use of political language."[9] The strategy is eloquently simple. Wright juxtaposes images of light and darkness, oppressor and oppressed. The American President and the Spanish Dictator, frozen in the ceremonious handshake and embrace of dignitaries, are illuminated by the glare of photographers' bulbs, "a shining circle of police," and airport searchlights reflecting from "Clean new bombers from America." Franco's promise that "all dark things / Will be hunted down" (*CP*, 122) and the sound of the American airplanes promise cooperation between the two nations to seek out the dark things in Spain.

The contrasting stanza identifies Antonio Machado, a poet eventually forced into exile because of his resistance to Franco's barbarism, with "a cave of silent children" and old men as inhabitants of the Spanish darkness. The epigraph, from Machado's contemporary Unamuno, "we die of cold, and not of darkness," becomes functional; there is a cold, sterile quality about the scene at the airfield, whereas the darkness features both a creative man who walks by moonlight and children, the hope of the future. Wine, with traditional Dionysian and Eucharistic connotations, "darkens in stone jars" and "sleeps in the mouths of old men" (*CP*, 122). As the wine darkens, it becomes richer. The political implication is that the health of the community rests with its ordinary citizens and creative outcasts, not with the leaders who conspire against them.

Franco has promised to hunt down these dark things, and as the bombers glide down to the field, America supplies the technology to implement that promise. With the embrace of the American military hero who brings planes to a Spanish general and dictator, the first two lines become a terrifying thesis about exporting repression: "The American hero must triumph over / The forces of darkness" (*CP*, 121). Exact phrasing and line division lead us to expect a positive victory in the first line, but the values aligned with the dark in this poem make it clear that the American hero may learn from the dictator how to turn the harsh light of authority on the lifeblood of the community, the private citizens.

Brilliant as it is, "Eisenhower's Visit" is less typical of Wright's new kind of political poem than "Having Lost My Sons, I Confront the Wreckage of the Moon: Christmas 1960," "Two Poems About President Harding," or "Stages on a Journey Westward." In these, the force of politics on the poet's own personality is profoundly felt, and the result of that pressure is rage at the inability of the individual of good will to change the conditions that threaten the traditions behind our political system. The poems about Harding are a qualified tribute to a mediocre politician, one who, in words Wright attributes to one of the president's friends, "lacks mentality."

An extremely popular executive, Harding favored business interests, and in the language of his campaign manager Harry Daugherty, "look[ed] like a president." Elected by a landslide in 1920, his administration scored minor victories in isolationist foreign policy and protectionist economic legislation, some of which should be credited to Secretary of State Charles Evans Hughes. The administration was plagued by scandals, most notably allegations of "fixing" in the Department of Justice, thievery by the director of the Veteran's Bureau and the suicide of his assistant, and the Teapot Dome and Elk Hills affairs. While the press created the image of fine president, Harding was unaware of the major scandals and inept in dealing with the minor ones he did learn about.

In "His Death," Wright sympathizes with the "vaguely stunned smile / Of a lucky man" (*CP*, 119) who found himself in a responsible position, who wanted to be known as "honest" and "helpful": "I am drunk this evening in 1961, / In a jag for my countryman / Who died of crabmeat on his way back from Alaska" (*CP*, 120). The "joke" about the crabmeat is an historically inaccurate, if popular, legend. The exact cause of Harding's death remains a mystery, and one writer went so far as to claim he was poisoned by his wife. The most credible explanation is a series of heart attacks.

The poet in 1961 must recognize, in his drunkenness, his political and cultural ties with the president who has become a public joke, but who was privately a victim of his position: "He died in public. He claimed the secret right / To be ashamed" (*CP*, 120). The separation of the public from the private Harding may refer to the president's grief over the betrayals. Just before his death, Harding asked Herbert Hoover to advise him about making public what he knew about the scandals, but he died before he could reach a decision. At any rate, Wright prefers his own arbitrary judgment, "Yet he was beautiful, he was the snowfall / Turned to white stallions standing still / Under dark elm trees" (*CP*, 120), over the public image of Harding as a bumpkin. This sympathetic account of a mediocre public man does not persuade us because nothing but Harding's essential good will substantiates it in the poem.

"His Tomb in Ohio" uses rhyme to contrast the ostentatious tomb of "our fellow citizen" with the disrespect Harding now commands. His succesors, Coolidge and Hoover, came to the dedication to "snivel about his broken heart," then "crept away / By night" (*CP*, 121), and the ugly tomb is now a hiding place for clandestine lovers and thieves, or an embarrassment to observers who have forgotten, if they ever knew, the man it was supposed to commemorate. In one of his increasingly frequent self-references, Wright mentions Minnegan Leonard, the brother who was feared drowned in "A Note Left in Jimmy Leonard's Shack," as typical of those who do not care about Harding or history or American civilization. Minnegan "half-believes / In God, and the poolroom goes dark" (*CP*, 121).

Wright's rage at the American skill in neglecting the past prompts a furious, hardly lyrical, outburst of personal emotion that recalls Swift's use of rhyme for satiric effects:

America goes on, goes on
Laughing, and Harding was a fool.
Even his big pretentious stone
Lays him bare to ridicule.
I know it. But don't look at me.
By God, I didn't start this mess.
Whatever moon and rain may be,
The hearts of men are merciless.
(*CP*, 121)

Generalizing the ironies of Harding's public life and reputation, Wright condemns the unforgiving nature of humanity and America's refusal to learn from the errors of the past. The blame can be a public one; the tomb is ours, and we ignore the lessons of history. Yet individuals must take a share of the blame, and Wright implicates himself as one of those who deny responsibility. The colloquial "don't look at me" and "I didn't start this mess," while they apparently disclaim personal responsibility for the mess we have made of history, finally implicate the poet in a willful abdication of responsibility for the past, and by extension, the present.

The need to define one's self in relation to geography and the cultural traditions implicit in locations organizes "Stages on a Journey Westward." In "Having Lost My Sons," the poet feels "lost in the beautiful white ruins / Of America" (CP, 132), and the strategy of "Stages" helps Wright discover the roots of that loss. The other poem traces the causes for loss in personal grief, but in "Stages" the causes are explained by the relation between actual space and the dreams associated with each place. Those in the first part are personal and generally beneficient. Because he "began in Ohio," the poet dreams of horses finding security in barns and of economic hardships his father faced during the depression. If he has trouble seeing him in "the bread lines my father / Prowls," he is comforted by the protection his parent provided against the perils outside: "In 1932, grimy with machinery, he sang me / A lullaby of a goosegirl. / Outside the house, the slag heaps waited" (CP, 116). The father's song temporarily protected the child from the bleak economic reality with which the father had to contend.

The sequence is geographical rather than temporal, and in the second part, Wright is in Minnesota, where he lived when he wrote the poem. There, he dreams about being a solitary camper, and "The only human beings between me and the Pacific Ocean / Were old Indians, who wanted to kill me" (CP, 117). If this sounds a bit paranoid, the fear implicitly recognizes the complicity of those who have profited by the genocide and dispossession of the American Indians, a theme Wright would explore again in the "New Poems" section of *Collected Poems*. The nightmare of cultural reprisal is not a plea for the noble savage, for Wright contrasts the silent staring into the fire of the Indians with his own crouching over a campfire, and notices that "The blades of their hatchets are dirty with the grease / Of huge, silent buffaloes" (CP, 117). The Indians may have differed in degree from the white civilization's rapacity, but they too destroyed living things in the search for survival.

The third section is a waking dream in Nevada. The poet, drunk and cold from not having lit the stove, listens to snow howling "out of the abandoned prairies" and taking on human speech: "It sounds like the voices of bums and gamblers, / Rattling through the bare nineteenth-century whorehouses / In Nevada" (*CP,* 117). Wind and snow echo a past marked by transients who profited by the boom town, then went their ways.

In the final section, Wright stands in a graveyard with a defeated, "half-educated sheriff" from Washington, where he lived before moving to Minnesota. Poet and sheriff are drunk again, perhaps hiding from the despair "half-educated" people feel when they contemplate the American scene. The poet extends this retreat from reality to symbolic death when "I lie down between tombstones." Drinking is no escape from the past. Wright remembers other transients, "Miners [who] paused here on their way to Alaska. / Angry, they spaded their broken women's bodies / Into ditches of crabgrass" (*CP,* 117). Like the Ohio diggers in "Miners," these transients courted wrath and despair in the quest to harvest the riches of the earth, but their search for wealth destroyed the ones they loved and condemned them all to unremembered graves.

From all these scenes, Wright draws a frightening generalization about the fate and future of American civilization:

> At the bottom of the cliff
> America is over and done with.
> America,
> Plunged into the dark furrows
> Of the sea again.
>   (*CP,* 117)

Like everything he has seen and dreamed of, the American experience is transient. We have put down graves and a legacy of rapacity rather than roots. The reference to the sea as both destroyer and source of new life, like a furrow in a field, answers the despairing question of "As I step over a Puddle": "Where is the sea, that once solved the whole loneliness / Of the Midwest?" It is all around us, and it is within us.

The Branch Will Not Break articulates a general loss of faith in the political process, while recognizing that some means of governance must be found if we are to survive as a culture and as individuals. The individual may also try to make a separate peace with nature, and on this point Wright's attitude is more ambiguous and hopeful than it is on the political front.

Nature: The Strength of the Branch

In the first two books, Wright wrote nature poetry, but his attitude toward nature was ambivalent. In *The Branch Will Not Break,* this attitude becomes even more complex. One part of Wright wants to write in the romantic tradition and to see nature as a comforter and healer, as Whitman and Wordsworth did. By temperament a perceptive observer and recorder, he wanted to write poems that captured moments of inspiration and the awareness of the divine presence that scenes of natural beauty can create in us. "Today I Was So Happy, So I Made this Poem" represents a joyful instance of this intuition. After looking at the moon and watching a squirrel scamper, Wright comes to conclusions that are in mood and tone, if not in diction or idiom, identical with attitudes in Whitman:

> And I see that it is impossible to die.
> Each moment of time is a mountain.
> An eagle rejoices in the oak trees of heaven,
> Crying
> *This is what I wanted.*
>
> (*CP,* 133)

This radiant moment brings Wright logically to associate the magnitude of each instant of time with confidence in immortality. He blends the natural and the divine in an eagle, whose cry can be interpreted by the poet as a confirmation of his own happiness and of nature's capacity to respond to human aspirations.

Although Wright eagerly absorbed the romantic tradition and was sometimes able to express feelings like Wordsworth's affirmation of nature as the "guardian of my heart, and soul" in "Tintern Abbey," he also responded to more recent intellectual and literary currents. Most modern thinkers have been unable to sustain the optimism of Wordsworth or Whitman, and Wright was profoundly moved by the antipastoral strains of Hardy, Robinson, and Frost. Like most of his contemporaries, Wright could not sustain, until the final two volumes, the hope of "Today I Was So Happy," "Snowstorm in the Midwest," or the tribute to his goddaughter "Mary Bly." Instead, his poems record attempts to forge a viable link with nature, one honest enough to acknowledge personal mortality and yet able to sustain the private self.

Nature often reminds Wright of human imperfection. It remains an abiding source of beauty and comfort, but it also recalls attempts by the human race to subdue and exploit it. These sentiments probably originate in Wright's youth in an industial basin of great natural beauty. Many poems in this and the next collections record the tension between a mystical impulse and the recognition that human interaction with nature can rob it of its consoling powers.

The poem from which the title of the volume is taken, "Two Hangovers," exemplifies this dual recognition. Placed strategically at the center of the collection, the two sections offer contrasting variations on the traditional morning hymn. In "Number One" surreal imagery and personification transform all perceptions, because of the poet's condition, into emblems of mortality and disgust. The trees are bare, and the depression of the poet's youth is personified as "an old man / Counting his collection of bottle caps / In a tarpaper shack under the cold trees / Of my grave" (*CP*, 124). Economic impoverishment associated with death leads the poet to impose his mortal condition on the literal objects he sees: "all those old women beyond my window / Are hunching toward the graveyard" (*CP*, 124).

Until he awoke, Wright could dream of the beautiful in the utilitarian and of joy in mortality. Still drunk, he dreamed about "green butterflies" that tried to find diamonds in seams of coal and children who chased each other "for a game / Through the hills of fresh graves" (*CP*, 125). Waking, he can no longer bring reality into conformity with human aspirations. The personified sun is as drunk as the poet, and when it "staggers in," "his big stupid face" falls on the stove. The sun is "mumbling Hungarian," presumably an unintelligible language for a poet writing in American English, and thus represents one of Wright's characteristic attitudes toward nature: it has a language with which to speak, but it does not speak intelligibly and we are not competent receivers. The fact that it can speak, but that we cannot understand, compounds our feeling of alienation. Because of these recognitions, a sparrow's song "of the Hanna Coal Co. and the dead moon" summons impressions of dying emotions and imaginations as well as economic exploitation of nature. This combination of perceptions produces disgust and the desire to retreat from what the poet is forced to recognize about our alienation from nature: "Ah, turn it off."

If the several images of "Number One" led to despair, a single image in "Number Two: I Try to Waken and Greet the World Once Again" leads to simple but transcendent joy. The drab sparrow of the first hangover is replaced by a "brilliant" and feisty blue jay springing up and down on a slender branch. Natural beauty and human delight now fuse in an exquisite synthesis:

> I laugh, as I see him abandon himself
> To entire delight, for he knows as well as I do
> That the branch will not break.
>
> (*CP,* 125)

The jay's instinctive faith in the power of the branch to support him offers the poet a symbol for both an ethical and an aesthetic idea. The world we inhabit is filled with occasions for delight and despair, as suggested by the vertical motion of the branch. What gives us the courage to continue and the joy to make that continuation worthwhile is faith that our progess through life, though perilous, is sustained by a connection to nature, a branch that will not break. Our proper reaction to that faith is joy, and the best human reaction to the perils of emotional life is delight in the process itself. Wright's symbol has aesthetic implications, too. The randomness of the bird's motion is like the freedoms the poet now claims for his art, but there remains the connectedness of things, the branch to the tree and the poem to a new kind of formal, organic control.

The strategy of arrangement, the final emphasis on the jay, and the concise imagery indicate that the hopeful view is the preferred one in "Two Hangovers." A similar plan organizes the entire collection. With the exception of "The Jewel," an insistence on the authenticity of a private, secret self in which "My bones turn to dark emeralds" (*CP,* 114) the nature poems leading up to "Two Hangovers" concentrate on the despair occasioned when nature reminds us of the failure of human stewardship. "In the Face of Hatred" and "Fear is What Quickens Me" sympathize with the plight of wild animals, especially those "our fathers killed in America." In the latter, the poet shares the animals' terror. While they were hunted by our ancestors, they "stared about wildly" and the poet, fully aware of his separation from "the deer / In this northern field," also "look[s] about wildly" (*CP,* 115). The deer are able to deal with the loss of the moon, Wright's consistent symbol for love and imagination, but the poet becomes suspicious of the "tall woman" he sees and the rabbits and doves he hears whispering together. Fear of his surroundings "quickens"

Wright by making him alert to his environment and alive in terror.

The "red shadow of steel mills" that symbolizes the ability of modern technology to obliterate our harmonious rapport with nature in "Twilights" is also the subject of the most pessimistic of the nature poems, "A Message Hidden in an Empty Wine Bottle that I Threw into a Gully of Maple Trees One Night at an Indecent Hour." Emblems of death and the decline of the imagination are accompanied by references to technology: spiritually, and perhaps literally, dead women dance "around a fire / By a pond of creosote and waste water" (*CP,* 115) while blast furnaces sneak "across the pits of strip mines / To steal grapes / In heaven" (*CP,* 116). As a result of these impressions, the poet recognizes his own loneliness, then reaches for the moon, only to be thwarted by the shadows of the blast furnaces:

> Nobody else knows I am here.
> All right.
> Come out, come out, I am dying.
> I am growing old.
> An owl rises
> From the cutter bar
> Of a hayrake.
>
> (*CP,* 116)

As he resigns himself to literal and spiritual death by echoing a phrase from a child's game of hide-and-seek, the only consoling image is the ascent of the owl. Even though real hayrakes do not have cutter bars, the effect is to suggest an escape by a natural creature from human implements that simplify harvesting, but, like many inventions, can estrange us from our world.

As Stitt has suggested,[10] the general plan of the volume is to follow "Two Hangovers" with poems in which nature provides consolation and blessing to human kind, although "In the Cold House," "Rain," and "Arriving in the Country Again" recapture the more pessimistic moods of "Message." In "American Wedding," a hibernation like that of animals is proposed as an acceptable alternative to the disappointed hopes of a young wife. That consolation does not quite convince, but Wright's treatment of a literal hibernation, in "March," recalls Williams's springtime lyrics as an affirmation in spite of the precariousness of all life. After the winter's sleep, with its interruption of continuity, in the weather's "own good time," the bear triumphantly leads her cubs "Outside to the unfamiliar cities / Of moss" (*CP,* 128).

The healing power of nature, to restore the spirit wounded by artificial human conventions, is treated humorously in "A Prayer to Escape the Market Place," in which lying down under a tree is a
sanctuary from the deadlines of magazines and "the only duty that is
not death." Again the echo of Williams's mastery of the glimpse is
felt when Wright hears the flutter of a pheasant and turns "Only to
see him vanishing at the damp edge / Of the road" (*CP,* 133). A similar mood animates "Depressed by a Book of Bad Poetry, I Walk Toward an Unused Pasture and Invite the Insects to Join Me." The
poet-critic abandons the bad poems of men to hear the "clear sounds"
of natural creatures.

The most celebrated of Wright's nature poems is "A Blessing," a
small narrative of a visit by the poet and a friend to a pasture in
which two horses graze. Central to the poem is the welcome the po-
nies offer the intruding men, and by inference the discovery that human beings can still be welcome in nature: "they can hardly contain
their happiness / That we have come" (*CP,* 135). The poet is
delighted by their friendliness and lack of fear, and quickly feels an
appreciation for the beauty of the pony that "nuzzled my left hand."
His initial gratitude causes feelings almost like erotic love. He would
like to embrace the pony, and, as he strokes her ear, he notes that it
"is delicate as the skin over a girl's wrist." Suddenly—and it is on
this suddenness that the emotional and conceptual effects of the poem
depend—Wright discovers transcendent joy in the moment: "Suddenly I realize / That if I stepped out of my body I would
break / Into blossom" (*CP,* 135). This implies that at moments of
pure rapture, we discover not only joy, but a recognition of our harmony with creation, a harmony even humankind cannot entirely
destroy.

In the most optimistic of Wright's nature poems, nature welcomes
us as its wayward children. We enjoy moments of rapture, but even
then, as in "Beginning," we are reminded that our ultimate union
with nature is a fellowship of mortal beings: "The wheat leans back
toward its own darkness, / And I lean toward mine" (*CP,* 127). This
is not a superficial nature-worship, but an earned recognition of the
inevitable end of the process, conditioned by the awareness that our
harmony with nature, however imperfect, is what we have. It is the
branch, and it will not break. But we must learn the confidence and
receptivity to ride the branch well. Rough winds will buffet the
branch furiously, and many of these will form the subject matter in
Shall We Gather at the River, the "New Poems," and *Two Citizens.*

Chapter Four

"This Scattering Poem": *Shall We Gather at the River* and "New Poems"

In *The Branch Will Not Break* Wright grew in technique and theme, and his was quickly recognized as a distinctive voice among the postmodern poets. In the next volume as well as the thirty-three new poems he included in *Collected Poems,* he consolidated the experiments of the first stage of his artistic growth. Written at the height of his creative power and expressing confident technical control, *Shall We Gather at the River* contains many of Wright's most successful poems.

These poems should be viewed as formal refinements of the experiments with open forms in the previous volume, but they do not merely repeat the author's achievements. Wright expands the scope of the individual poem. Although several balance a revealing image against a sudden emotional judgment, a practice he had perfected in *The Branch Will Not Break,* some of the more intriguing from a technical standpoint use multiple images or situations, often in violent contrast with one another, and frequently organized as independent, numbered sections of a single poem. Examples of this attempt at greater scope include "The Minneapolis Poem," "A Secret Gratitude," "Poems to a Brown Cricket," and "Many of Our Waters: Variations on a Poem by a Black Child." The connections among the sections, in both subject matter and tone, are imaginative rather than narrative or overtly logical, and the poems usually require that the reader move freely in time, space, and attitude with the poet.

Wright continues to question the craft of the poet. He had raised this issue in each previous volume, but the temper of the question now takes on greater intensity. Again, the repudiates his own past poems and, in "Many of Our Waters," accuses himself of "slicking into my own words / The beautiful language of my friends" (*CP,* 212), or of writing derivative poems, but the questioning in these collections has psychological implications as well. Wright now ques-

tions his motives as an artist, as well as the communicative impetus
for poetry in general.

"Inscription for the Tank," in *Shall We Gather at the River*, addresses the popular mode of poetry as confession. Wright ponders the
risks of his special kind of personal poetry by contrasting his own art
with a more primitive form, *graffiti*. The poem reflects on the permanence art can achieve and the unique risk that permanence entails.
The poet is astonished by the impact recording a commonplace can
have:

> My life was never so precious
> To me as now.
> I gape unbelieving at those two lines
> Of my words, caught and frisked naked.
>   (*CP*, 142)

What startles poet and reader is the permanent shape this universal
thought has suddenly taken. There is a commitment here, the kind
we do not make when we merely verbalize a feeling, and yet the impulse to communicate our innermost feelings is probably very similar
to the one that causes prisoners to scribble inscriptions on the walls of
cells. The difference is that Wright, having crafted his feelings into a
line of poetry, must accept responsibility—to himself and to poster-
ity—for those feelings. One instinct is to wish that he had resisted
the impulse to communicate this insight, perhaps to have read the
feelings of a prophet or another poet or "anyone, anyone." It would
be possible to escape the consequences of feelings someone else expressed, but the poet is permanently responsible for his own formula-
tion: "But I wrote down mine, and now / I must read them forever"
(*CP*, 142).

Significantly, the crucial lines, repeated with the added conjunc-
tion "But" in "In Terror of Hospital Bills," echo, perhaps uncon-
sciously, a speech in Shakespeare's *Richard III*. Trying to console Lord
Stanley after his ominous dream and shortly to be himself deceived,
then executed, by the ambitious Protector, Lord Hastings declares, "I
hold my life as dear as yours, / And never, I do protest, / Was it so
precious to me as 'tis now" (3.2.77–79). It is unlikely that Wright
intended to allude to Shakespeare's lines, but this eloquent sentiment
of a character unwilling to compromise principle for expediency or
even survival undoubtedly lodged itself in the prodigious memory of
the American poet.

One concern of any artist who tends toward confession or self-revelation is that his emotions, which seem so profound at the moment, will prove trivial. Another is a psychological fear of revealing the secret self, of violating the privacy everyone needs:

> Of all my lives, the one most secret to me,
> Folded deep in a book never written,
> Locked up in the dream of a still place,
> I have blurted out.
>
> (*CP*, 142)

The conflict between professional or exhibitionistic tendencies and the need for privacy creates special vulnerability for confessional or expressive artists. While art reveals our inner selves to us, it also can lead to statements in which we may have to risk more than we are prepared to risk.

Wright also expresses reservations about art as artifice. He frets in "Many of Our Waters" over the "mangled figures of speech" of some New York poets and wishes in "Late November in a Field" that his own poems were less artificial: "I have nothing to ask a blessing for / Except these words. / I wish they were / Grass." (*CP*, 152).

These doubts about the purpose and effect of poems provide some occasions for humor in the "New Poems." He remembers his department chairman Ray Livingston who defined hell as "the difficult, the dazzling / Hendecasyllabic" (*CP*, 199), a form practiced by Catullus and Tennyson. Using rhyme for devastating satiric effects in "To a Dead Drunk," Wright charges that poetry in the modern world has practical value as fuel for academics:

> But someone whose triumphant name
> Is Lyndon Fink Jane Adam Smith
> Will pounce on your forgotten name
> To write a dissertation with.
>
> (*CP*, 190)

The wordplay implies that the academic will make his ridiculous name famous by exploiting the forgotten name of the creative person.

In some "New Poems," his doubts about the compatibility of poetry with modern life lead the poet to take the offensive. Anticipating indifference or hostility to the innovative poetics of his recent work, Wright occasionally antagonizes the reader in advance. In "Katy

Did," he uses Ohio vernacular to challenge the reader, not once but twice, to "Put that / In your pipe" (*CP*, 204–5). More aggressively, he alienates the unsympathetic reader in "Many of Our Waters":

> If you do not care one way or another about
> The preceding lines,
> Please do not go on listening
> On any account of mine.
> Please leave the poem.
> Thank you.
>
> (*CP*, 207)

One result of these doubts about the motives for, and impact of, his work is that Wright continued, even while he gained respect as a leader in contemporary poetry, to innovate and to grow. His was not an art that could be complacent, for the artist's doubts about what he was doing forced him to continue to experiment. An immediate result is a wider variety of styles and attitudes than his previous collections have exhibited, from the sarcastic in "To a Dead Drunk" to the ironic monologue "A Mad Song for William S. Carpenter," to the mode of prayer that dominates *Shall We Gather at the River*.

Many Rivers, Many Prayers

Several mysteries surround *Shall We Gather at the River*, not the least of which is the enigmatic title. Unlike the prevous volumes, in which the title was a line from or the title of a poem, this is a reference to an evangelical hymn. Yet Wright's title is not a question, like the hymn with its invitation to baptism, but a declaration. Wright intends his river to refer specifically to the Ohio of his youth, but it is not a river we would associate with purification. "Three Sentences for a Dead Swan" describes the river as a "Tar and chemical strangled tomb" that denies any promise of resurrection. It is "no tomb to / Rise from the dead / From" (*CP*, 156). By contrast, "In Response to the Rumor that the Oldest Whorehouse in Wheeling, West Virginia, Has Been Condemned" sees the Ohio as the location of a perverse resurrection for prostitutes. In "Humming a Tune for an Old Lady in West Virginia," the river yields up broken bodies, but promises no resurrection. "Many of Our Waters" treats the capacity of language to mock the reality it represents. Now resigned to returning to "my own river," "My rotted Ohio," Wright has recently learned the meaning of the word *Ohio* in the Winnebago language; it means "beautiful river."

Many waterways provide locations in *Shall We Gather at the River.* The Red River in North Dakota rises "To Flood Stage Again." The Mississippi is a grave for the unfortunates of "The Minneapolis Poem." The contaminated Ohio is James Wright's own river, but it represents all the waters we have polluted until we have turned nature into an enemy. It is not our option, but our fate, to gather at the rivers. We must be immersed in the nature we have destroyed, just as we must acknowledge our brotherhood with the outcasts and rejects of our society. As Wright and one of his favorite poets, William Carlos Williams, see it, we must undergo a baptism of the imperfect, in the "filthy Passaic" or "the rotted Ohio," in order to begin our journey toward salvation.

A new attitude emerges in these poems, one consistent with the religious implications of the title of the collection. The poems are like prayers. They petition a deity for relief from, or understanding of, the loneliness that is consistently defined as the fundamental human condition. Zweig observes that the tone is consistently that of quiet prayers, sounded under the noises of the cities and fields in which they are spoken yet unsure whether they have reached too far, and Wright gave credibility to this thesis when he described his intent in *Shall We Gather at the River* as a movement from death to resurrection to death again, in order "to challenge death finally": "and I knew exactly what I was doing from the first syllable to the very last one."[1]

One of Wright's finest political poems, "Confession to J. Edgar Hoover," depends for its effects on ironic use of the mode of prayer. Wright sets the stage for a discussion of war with this realistic portrait, full of intimations of pity, fear, implicit violence, and futility:

> Hiding in the church of an abandoned stone,
> A Negro soldier
> Is flipping the pages of the Articles of War
> That he can't read.
>
> *(CP, 163)*

One of Wright's typical characters, the soldier is a victim of the military bureaucracy. He may be hiding from either the enemy or his comrades—we cannot be sure which. In either case, no code of military conduct will do him any good, because he cannot read it. His hiding place is not even a real sanctuary. The image does not picture the ruin of a cathedral, but a stone pressed into service as an apparent sanctuary.

This image sets the stage for the confession central to the poem. It is not a war poem, but a petition to the lifetime director of the F.B.I., and the soldier is not the confessant. His experience is the background for the confession of a speaker who admits sneaking "To pray with a sick tree" and devouring "the wing / Of a cloud." These acts, which suggest an appropriate reverence for nature, are like sins. They are done covertly, and penance must begin with confession.

The analogy with the soldier clarifies the inversion of values central to the poem. Like the soldier, the speaker is caught in a system he cannot understand. His instincts tell him that it is right to revere nature, but his rational judgment tells him that such reverence puts him at risk before Hoover, the high priest of technological surveillance. Wright amplifies the technological implications of Hoover's kingdom through another set of images:

> I labor to die, father,
> I ride the great stones,
> I hide under stars and maples,
> And yet I cannot find my own face.
> In the mountains of blast furnaces,
> The trees turn their backs on me.
>   (*CP,* 163)

In our collective religion of substituting engineering technology, or blast furnaces, for nature, or mountains, we lose our identity and court a suicidal loss of harmony with the world around us. Because we have rejected nature, it seems to turn its back on us, and the speaker loses his sense of authentic being. Having lost that sense, he inappropriately turns to the culture that has alienated him to be forgiven. Seeking Hoover's blessing, the speaker pleads, "Father, forgive me. / I did not know what I was doing" (*CP,* 164). Before an alienating social system, Wright here implies through both dramatic and verbal irony that we need an excuse like temporary insanity to justify cherishing nature.

Whereas Wright uses the traditional ironic device of speaking through a persona whose views he intends the reader to reject in "Confession," he speaks in a more personal voice in most of the poems. This voice is heard in a series of earnest prayers to the muse of this collection.

After the enigmatic title, the second mystery of *Shall We Gather* is the identity of Jenny. The book is dedicated to her without explanation, but the central and final poems, "Speak" and "To the Muse," along with "The Idea of the Good," the first of the "New Poems," and "October Ghosts," in *Two Citizens,* identify Jenny as an Ohio prostitute and as Wright's muse. In "The Idea of the Good," Wright addresses her as a secret sharer, against those readers who will not understand or care about their secret:

> Jenny, I gave you that unhappy
> Book that nobody knows but you
> And me, so give me
> A little life back. . . .
> Nobody else will follow
> This poem but you,
> But I don't care.
> By precious secret, how
> Could they know
> You or me?
>
> (*CP,* 173)

As in several "New Poems," Wright challenges his readers and assumes that most have ignored *Shall We Gather at the River.* He asks his tainted muse to restore his life, or to give him some token (an owl's feather) of their lost love. All he can advise for Jenny, or for himself, or for anyone suffering the loneliness we share, is "Patience." This will be a central theme in his subsequent poems.

If "The Idea of the Good" is a plea to Jenny to save the poet by sharing his love as well as his secret, "To the Muse" petitions her to allow the poet to save his "Muse of black sand" from the river itself. She now inhabits "the suckhole, the south face / Of the Powhatan pit" (*CP,* 168) but the poet encourages her to undergo the pain—it "hurts / Like nothing I know"—of an operation to remove fluid from her lungs. Nathan infers from the operation that Jenny is a "real girl whom he early loved and who apparently committed suicide," whereas Costello considers her an embodiment of his "idea of the failing heartland" and a "casualty of the love-starved land." Wright himself offered conflicting identifications. While explaining his sense of the structure of the book, he mentioned an autobiographical intention: "I was trying to write about a girl I was in love with who has been dead a long time. I was trying to sing with her." Earlier in the

interview, he quoted with delight the digression from book 9, chapter 8, of *Tristram Shandy* in which Sterne introduces an unidentified
"my dear *Jenny!*" to comment on the passage of time. Sterne's digression concludes with a tone that resonates in Wright's poems about
Jenny: "—Heaven have mercy upon us both!" Wright's delight in
Sterne's coy refusal to identify Jenny raises questions about his autobiographical identification of his muse.[2]

The most plausible explanation is that Jenny is a fictional composite containing elements from Wright's memory, fantasy, and imagination. Certainly she is more important as a symbol in his poems
than as a biographical figure. Her Ohio reminds one of the Styx, for
Wright concedes. "I know / The place where you lie. / I admit everything" (*CP*, 169), but he prays that Jenny allow him to "lead you
back to this world" (*CP*, 168). Still, the world to which he would
restore the fallen muse is one in which the constant is pain, "And you
bear it" (*CP*, 168).

This awareness of the pain all living beings must bear in order to
live and to love brings the poet to reflect on his responsibility for the
state of the world in ways that contrast with the abdication of responsibility in "Two Poems About President Harding":

> Oh Jenny,
> I wish to God I had made this world, this scurvy
> And disastrous place. I
> Didn't, I can't bear it
> Either, I don't blame you, sleeping down there.
>   (*CP*, 168–69)

Whereas in the Harding poem he disclaimed responsibility by saying
"I didn't start this mess," he now wishes that he could accept blame
for the world that has failed Jenny. Even though he cannot contemplate a better world of his own making, he wishes that this flawed
world were a result of some human intention—so that someone could
take responsibility for its failures—rather than of some incomprehensible design or accident.

"Speak," the first poem about Jenny, is placed strategically at the
center of *Shall We Gather*. It is simultaneously a defense of the poetics
of the book and a literal prayer seeking God's approval for Wright's
attitude toward society's outcasts. Twice Wright defends his conversational, understated style: "To speak in a flat voice / Is all that I can

do" (*CP*, 149), but the flat voice is more complicated than it seems. The poem combines styles from journalism, cryptic narrative, revivalist rhetoric, Biblical allusion, and prayer. Wright uses simple diction, but the effects of "Speak" are highly studied.

Jenny enters Wright's poetry as a specific example of frustrated hope. The poet has asked for God and for her everywhere, but has learned that the despairing observation of Ecclesiastes (9.11) is proved by experience: "Then I returned rebuffed / And saw under the sun / The race is not to the swift / Nor the battle won" (*CP*, 149). One example is boxer Sonny Liston, who, Wright believes, took a dive in his loss to Cassius Clay. Another is Ernie Doty, who is drunk "In hell again." The most important is of course Jenny:

> And Jenny, oh my Jenny
> Whom I love, rhyme be damned,
> Has broken her spare beauty
> In a whorehouse old.
> She left her new baby
> In a bus-station can
> And sprightly danced away
> Through Jacksontown.
>
> (*CP*, 149–50)

Wright does not excuse Jenny's conduct, but loves her in spite of it. Her "sprightly" reaction to infanticide may tax the reader's sympathy, but Wright wants us to see her as a victim of a loveless society. He encourages this by rhetorical contrasts: an archaic "oh"; an inversion implying that the brothel is more permanent than people; and enigmatic phrases like "spare beauty," suggesting both excess and sparse, in either case wasted.

The reader's attention is riveted by the modest curse against rhyme, seemingly arbitrary and of questionable relevance in this sympathetic account of Jenny. Upon reflection, the alert reader will discover that Wright has used approximate rhymes throughout the poem until now, yet he refuses to rhyme one of the easier English words, *old*. He completes this rhetorical ploy by returning to approximate rhyme in the rest of the poem, so the complaint is not against rhyme, but against the type of decorum that requires poets to uphold convention and respectable people to despise whores who abandon their offspring. Wright challenges this kind of respectability by making the flawed girl his muse.

A literal prayer for divine approval ends the poem. The credentials Wright can place before his creator are love for the Jennys, the unwanted and rejected of the world. He prays for some sign that this has been the correct moral choice:

> Lord, I have loved Thy cursed,
> The beauty of Thy house;
> Come down. Come down. Why dost
> Thou hide thy face?
>
> (*CP*, 150)

"Speak" is Wright's version of the Book of Job, an inquiry into the nature of the moral life and a desperate request for divine sanction of the choices existential man must make. Like most of the prayers in *Shall We Gather at the River*, it is not answered.

Mystery about the fate of prostitutes is also the subject of the meditation "In Response to a Rumor that the Oldest Whorehouse in Wheeling, West Virginia, Has Been Condemned." Wright ponders his childhood perception of the constant procession of whores into and out of the river as a perverse baptism and resurrection. Now, he still cannot understand: "I do not know how it was / They could drown every evening" (*CP*, 165). He can, however, express the despair from which the river offered contaminated sanctuary:

> For the river at Wheeling, West Virginia,
> Has only two shores:
> The one in hell, the other
> In Bridgeport, Ohio.
>
> And nobody would commit suicide, only
> To find beyond death
> Bridgeport, Ohio.
>
> (*CP*, 166)

Wright's wit identifies hell as both sides of his polluted river. Like the whores, we are caught between versions of hell, and what some existentialists term the final option to assert the self, suicide, is rendered by this logic a ridiculous choice.

Another river, again a tomb, and a population of outcasts including whores from Chicago, contribute to the most despairing, and technically dazzling, of Wright's prayers. "The Minneapolis Poem" consists of seven independent reflections on the failure of life in the modern City. Auden's judgment, in the preface to *The Green Wall*, that Wright's characters are "the City's passive victims," had proved absolutely true within little more than a decade. Wright is no longer an advocate for the victims; he has identified his concerns and fears completely with theirs. This identification with the nameless is a profound questioning of the sociological and institutional ties that bind human beings into a community. The seemingly fragmented organization of "The Minneapolis Poem" expresses perfectly its central theme, the hopelessness, terror, violence, and indifference at the heart of the modern City.

Wright observes, comments on, and participates in the alienation that now takes the place of community. Standing "By Nicollet Island," a suitably isolated location for a poem about the failure of the community, Wright mourns the nameless and numberless old men who committed suicide in the river, and wonders, "How does the city keep lists of its fathers / Who have no names?" (*CP,* 140). The police, symbolizing the indifference of authority, turn in the bodies (Wright uses the medical term *cadavers* to suggest experimental uses for the city's fathers) to anonymity "somewhere," and the only community afforded these citizens is death. Despite his desire to console them, Wright can wish them only "good luck / And a warm grave" in contrast to the bad luck and cold winters they knew in Minneapolis.

The second section may be the most spectacular use Wright ever made of "the pure clear word." He isolates four groups, and there is no hope of their ever coming together as a community to reshape the fragmented City. Within the groups, fear or a sinister purpose dominates the individuals. "The Chippewa young men / Stab one another shrieking / Jesus Christ" (*CP,* 140). America's original citizens, aliens in the modern City, invoke the conqueror's god as a curse. Their bond is violent and self-destructive; they take out their wrath and frustration on one another, not on the oppressor. A group with a common purpose, "Split-lipped homosexuals limp in terror of assault" (*CP,* 140). Their common goal is to avoid persecution by the heterosexual majority, but their injuries show how unsuccessful they have been. The middle class is represented when, "High school backfields search under benches / Near the Post Office" (*CP,* 140). That we never know what they are looking for implies a sinister purpose, and these are not the "suicidally beautiful" football players of "Autumn Begins in Martins Ferry, Ohio": "Their faces are the rich / Raw bacon without eyes" (*CP*, 140). The most skilled athletes, representing the schools that must produce the leaders of the future, are blind searchers, united in what seems to be a malevolent quest. The elite are here too: "The Walker Art Center crowd stare / At the Guthrie Theater" (*CP*, 140). Unlike the other groups, this one expresses no purpose, unless it be competition among the artistic elite. Their response to America's cultural landmarks is apathetic and pointless. The central themes of the section are that no organization of these groups into a unified social purpose is possible, and that there is no creative life in any of them.

The next two sections treat other outcasts from the City. The prostitutes, unlike Jenny, have developed instincts to cope with authority by recognizing the "supposed patron" who is really a policeman. The protective evolution of these whores leads Wright to visually effective, if oversimplified and paranoid, images for "the insolence of office," a theme that intrigued him when he wrote about Dickens:

> A cop's palm
> Is a roach dangling down the scorched fangs
> Of a light bulb.
> The soul of a cop's eyes
> Is an eternity of Sunday daybreak in the suburbs
> Of Juárez, Mexico.
>
> (*CP*, 140)

James Wright was too kind and generous a man to have believed this of individual police officers, but his rhetoric forces him into overstatement. Because the strategy of the poem dictates a perpetual conflict between authority and the victims of the City, Wright forgot for much of *Shall We Gather at the River* that police and other officials are people too. It was a simplification symptomatic of the last years of the 1960s, but an intellectual like Wright could have avoided it.

In the fourth section, the tone shifts toward escape and resurrection. More victims of the failure of the human community, the "legless beggars" are "gone," but they were "carried away / By white birds" (*CP*, 140). This image will provide the poet with his own hope for escape in section seven. Although a death image, it implies that death is also an escape from the despair of the modern City. Wright hints ironically at resurrection of the body, and his sympathy with these victims contrasts with the hope for a warm grave in section one: "I think of poor men astonished to waken / Exposed in broad daylight by the blade / Of a strange plough" (*CP*, 141). While this is hardly a consoling prediction, it does contain waking and astonishment, as opposed to dehumanizing technologies like the Artificial Limbs Exchange, which has been rendered superfluous by the death of the beggars. Now "gutted / And sown with lime," this misery industry no longer blights the landscape.

The only happy inhabitants of this metropolis are automobiles, upon which the owners lavish more care than on their fellow citizens, and which express the most positive emotions in "The Minneapolis Poem" as they "Consent with a mutter of high good humor" to rest between commuting trips. With this personification, Wright summarizes another theme: alienation and technology have created conditions that render human happiness and community impossible, and whatever figurative contentment is left belongs to the devices we have created to serve us, but which have become our masters. This personification leads to a turning point in which Wright expresses a paranoia that is the direct result of alienation: "There are men in this city who labor dawn after dawn / To sell me my death" (*CP*, 141).

Wright does not identify these enemies precisely, but many candidates come to mind within the poem. The police and other authorities, or perhaps their opposites, the street criminals who prey on the unfortunate and alienated, are surely among those who convert the dawn, a time of birth, into a time of death and victimization. If this fear sounds paranoid, it is also an indictment of the self, for to sell someone his death requires that the buyer actively participate in the transaction.

With this revelation that one cannot be simply a sympathetic observer of the cycle of destruction that makes up our collective identity, Wright turns from deep image to his personal mode of prayer. In the sixth section, he rejects Minneapolis, a synecdoche for all the failed communities, as a resting place for "my poor brother my body," but with this rejection he asserts that a self independent of material being may transcend death. Wright strategically invokes the patron of American poets, "The old man Walt Whitman our countryman / Is now in America our country / Dead" (*CP*, 141). This allusion recalls the death not only of the spokesman of democracy who is now one with the beggars and the suicides, but of the dream his poetry represented, of a culture inclusive enough to nourish the growth of all its citizens. Wright's carefully dislocated syntax reveals that what is mourned is not only the passing of Whitman, but that of the America he knew, loved, and created.

The curious consolation is that "he was not buried in Minneapolis / At least" (*CP*, 141). Whitman was spared the ignominy of being placed at rest in the modern city, and Wright turns to overt prayer that he may share this modest blessing: "And no more may I be / Please God" (*CP*, 141). This syntax implies both a petition to God for the granting of a wish and a submission to divine Will; the petition can be read, "If it please God."

"The Minneapolis Poem" concludes with Wright's prayer to become a seed, an image that completes the hope for resurrection in section four. He wants to be carried, like the beggars, by "some great white bird unknown to the police," and thus to escape the entrapment that threatens the prostitutes in section three and the indifference with which the suicides are treated in section one. By rejecting the City, Wright offers a jaded proletarian version of the return to nature of the romantics. Rather than being buried in Minneapolis, his essential self would be "Stored with the secrets of the wheat and the mysterious lives / Of the unnamed poor" (*CP*, 141). An eternal community of the nameless is envisioned and the image of wheat suggests vitality and regeneration among the unwanted citizens of America. As an alternative to the failed life of the City, the end of "The Minneapolis Poem" is not intellectually persuasive, but it is a profoundly moving expression of anguish at the failure of basic human institutions to respond to human needs. It is both a prayer for personal deliverance and a diagnosis of the failure of modern American civilization.

Economics, Alienation, and the Prodigal Son

While writing the poems collected in *Shall We Gather,* Wright placed new emphasis on economic conditions as a source of alienation. Long concerned with the suffering of outcasts, he found a viable theme in the degree to which the distribution of money affects the self-defining choices we must make. Although he was not an economic theorist, Wright was a citizen who knew something about the ordinary marketplace. As a poet, he saw that a market economy profoundly affects the content of our moral lives. The attrition of spirit and the essential self, always a central concern in his works, could in some measure be traced to external economic conditions.

Borrowing and lending compromise the self in two "New Poems,"

"The Offense" and "To a Friendly Dun." The former recollects stimulating disagreements about literature and society between Wright and Ray Livingston at Macalester College, but the offense is that he allowed Ray to loan him five dollars he did not really need. Although it is a trivial matter between friends, the poet feels that a wedge was driven into their friendship: "Why did you do it, Ray?" Livingston's generosity is not the principal question here. What Wright wonders is, why did he accept the sum, when conversation with Ray was the real capital of their friendship? "To a Friendly Dun" recalls an evening when the hungry poet shared a poor meal, then, touched by their mutual despair, lent his acquaintance two hundred fifty dollars, "And I would rather be dead than ask him / To pay me back" (*CP*, 201). Wright's anger gives way to rage as he considers the cheap price he, and the recipient, attached to his good works. The poet knows he alone is responsible for the gesture and for the ethical value he attaches to it, but the poem makes the point that material goods can be easy substitutes for giving the self.

Unburdened by the rhetorical excesses of this poem, "In Terror of Hospital Bills" and others in *Shall We Gather* assess the choices forced on us by lack of money. Contemplating the bleakest prospects, "alone, / And frightened, knowing how soon / I will waken a poor man" (*CP*, 143), the poet considers possible strategies for begging money, if it should come to that. His secret self would be betrayed by the expedient of begging, so the choice is between survival and integrity. The impulse to survive cannot be set aside, as Wright realizes when he repeats the Shakespearian lines from "Inscription for the Tank," "my life was never so precious / To me as now" (*CP*, 143). The compromises forced upon him by economics would be almost as debasing as the loss of life itself. He would become a refugee from civic authority by learning to "scent the police," or a living dead man learning to "sit or go blind, stay mute, be taken for dead." The dilemma is that these types of spiritual death may be forced upon him in order to protect his life, his "secret / Hounded and flayed" (*CP*, 143), from extinction.

In any society, possession of wealth can be confused with intrinsic worth. "Before a Cashier's Window in a Department Store" deals with a necessary corollary, that the individual's sense of self-worth can be intimidated by others' perception of one's economic circumstances. The cashier and manager seem to conspire against the poet. He feels "pinned down / By debt" and by the merciless gaze of the manager who seems to be "Commending my flesh to the pity of the daws of God" (*CP,* 148). Wright suspects that the cashier, complacent in her "heaven of the beautiful," knows the fate of bums like him: "The bulldozers will scrape me up / After dark, behind / The officer's club" (*CP,* 148). There is no escape from the prison of debt except death, but Wright accepts this association with "the dark," one of his recurring metaphors for the condition of the poor.

The fourth section seems, on first reading, unrelated to the primary scene. Without introductory link, Wright portrays the oriental Tu Fu awakening on a battlefield to see women looting the corpses of soldiers, a scene reminiscent of Ransom's "Necrological." The scene establishes historical continuity for Wright's reception in the eyes of the cashier. Regardless of culture or historical time, humanity has always practiced economic savagery at the expense of the dignity of other persons.

Wright's theme, the despair of the self and the future that results from the lack of wealth in a materialist society, is tersely expressed in the final section:

> I am hungry. In two more days
> It will be spring. So this
> Is what it feels like.
>
> (*CP,* 149)

Spring, traditionally associated with hope and the future, promises more dread. Wright has accepted the cashier's version of his worth, really his own projection of value onto her, and this acceptance destroys any hope for the future.

"Gambling in Stateline, Nevada," a brilliant contrast of images in the manner of *The Branch Will Not Break,* speaks of the frenzy and despair to which the love of money drives us. The girl Rachel escaped across the border into California, but "died of bad luck." A woman, frenzied by winning and losing, "Has been beating a strange machine / In its face all day" (*CP,* 144). Wright steps outside, perhaps to enjoy natural beauty as an antidote to the frantic despair of the casino, and "I finger a worthless agate / In my pocket" (*CP,* 144). He too has lost in Stateline, but at least he has learned the value of the playing stone he retains. The brief but rich descriptions of western beauty hint that the poet will not die "of bad luck" because he has learned to value beauty over material gains.

Effective diagnoses of alienation, *Shall We Gather* and the "New Poems" form a quest for brotherhood and love. We have seen that love for the unfortunate is the redemptive theme of the Jenny poems, and the poems and prayers about alienation are balanced by an equally impressive number about the need for love, both erotic and fraternal, as the best antidote to despair.

"Many of Our Waters," Wright's most experimental poem, is marred by many flaws of arbitrary construction and unchecked irritability, but it is almost redeemed by the sheer rhetorical power of its emphasis on love. Its finest moment is section five, an account of a trip to the planetarium by the Wrights and Garnie Braxton, one of Anne's pupils who accepted James as a surrogate father and influenced their lives profoundly. From across a dangerous intersection, Garnie asks James, "Can Kinny come too? / I ain't got nothing but my brother" (*CP*, 210). In the excitement of the conversation and the possible danger to the boys, Garnie repeats that he has "nothing but my brother," and Wright suddenly realizes that the child has hit upon the most fundamental truth of all human relationships: "Neither have I, get the hell over here." Wright discovers that Garnie and Kinny are all each other has, but that if they will just "get the hell over here," they can be Wright's brothers too, despite differing racial and economic backgrounds.

Subtitled "Variations on a Poem by a Black Child," the poem is a tribute to the love Wright felt for Garnie and the wisdom of Garnie's insight, but it is dedicated to Wright's brother Jack. In the final section Wright addresses Jack directly by paraphrasing Garnie, "You're my brother at last, / And I don't have anything / Except my brother" (*CP*, 212), but he has also found that the only conditions under which personal freedom can survive are love and respect for the individuality of one another: "And how can I live my life / Unless you live yours?" (*CP*, 212). Whether the brother be a literal relative like Jack, or a fellow human being being like Garnie, accepting and cherishing his freedom is the only way to secure our own identity.

Erotic love can also ameliorate the alienation so characteristic of modern life, not only because eros brings people out of their prisons of self, but because the erotic in Wright, as in the Elizabethan and early Jacobean poets he admired, leads to spiritual love and an appreciation of the worth of the lover. This theme organizes "Poems to a Brown Cricket," in which the cricket symbolizes occasions for love Wright has felt throughout his life. He derives a heightened sense of himself from the fact that he was worthy of someone's love: "I don't care who loved me. / Somebody did, so I let myself alone" (*CP*, 166). He forgave himself his faults because he saw in the reflection of the women he loved his own better self.

Wright varies this theme in "So She Said," a memory of his respect for the hesitation of a lover who "knew me lonely so she took / My bare body into her bed" (*CP*, 187). His acceptance of her bashfulness will console him in his most terrifying hour:

> And when I lay me down to die
> Let me call back I might have used
> The woman of a girl who loved me
> Enough to let me let her lie
> Alone in her own loneliness,
> And mind her own good business.
>
> (*CP*, 187)

The poet is confident that both her love for him and the memory of sparing her his own demands in order to respect her wishes will authenticate his essential self in the face of death. His claim to virtue will be that he refrained from using another person to achieve his own ends.

While on a fellowship in 1965, Wright visited his parents in Martins Ferry. Several poems in *Shall We Gather* treat that rediscovery of his homeland, and such poems as "RIP" and "A Way to Make a Living" anticipate the reconciliation with Ohio and America that followed *Two Citizens*. Others develop the theme of love, even in the face of disappointed expectations, as the answer to despair. The two tributes to his father portray James's revised perspective on the "slave" to a factory who "tried to teach me kindness" in "At the Executed Murderer's Grave." "Youth" is a lovely tribute to the dignity of a provider who "worked too hard to read books," but who was able to keep the rage he must have felt during fifty years among "dumb honyaks" at Hazel-Atlas Glass away from the home he created for his family: "my brother and I do know / He came home as quiet as the evening" (*CP*, 154). This appreciation of the father's quiet virtue is all the more powerful because the poem is really Wright's attempt to come to terms with the fact that his father has grown old, and must soon die.

The same lament animates "Two Postures Beside a Fire." Wright now appreciates the support his father gave him in his despair. He sees serene beauty in the repose of this old man who "broke stones, / Wrestled and mastered great machines" to provide him with a home. His own signs of age are ugly and nervous, in contrast with the beauty of the sleeping parent. Wright feels that his life has been a failure by contrast with the achievements of this uncomplicated, decent man:

> He is proud of me, believing
> I have done strong things among men and become a man
> Of place among men of place in the large cities.
> I will not waken him.
> I have come home alone, without wife or child
> To delight him.
>
> (*CP,* 161)

In the emotional crises surrounding Wright's life at this time—divorce, separation from his sons, and academic disappointments at Minnesota—his father's love and pride sustain him, and the decision not to impose his disappointments on his father is one way to reciprocate his love.

Shortly before he visited Ohio, Wright had written "Willy Lyons," his first and most popular poem of reconciliation with his birthplace. He later explained that he wrote the poem in Minnesota, after being informed by Jack of his Uncle William's death.[3] Lyons was a skilled craftsman and local character in both dress and attitude, whom Wright would remember again in "Chilblain." "Willy Lyons" anticipates the tone of reconciliation in the poems about Wright's father, but ends with the alienation characteristic of many of the Minneapolis poems: "Willy, and John [Willy's brother], whose life and art, if any, / I never knew" (*CP,* 159). In its attempt to console his mother's grief, "Willy Lyons" is an overt statement of Wright's belief in the transcendent world: "It is nothing to mourn for. / It is the other world" (*CP,* 158–159). He recognizes that weeping serves his mother's needs, but the poem reminds her that her brother has been welcomed in the "other world" where he "planes limber trees by the waters," thus extending into eternity the art that his nephew never knew, but recognized as essential to making Willy the man he was.

These poems begin the process of Wright's reconciliation with his native place, with which he had struggled in the earlier books. He would continue to explore his attitudes toward America in *Two Citizens.* Before undertaking this theme, Wright would reevaluate his

feelings about nature, and this contributes one of the central concerns
of the "New Poems."

Nature and the Human Creature

Shortly before his death, Wright explained why he always considered himself a nature poet:

I care very much about the living world, the organic and the inorganic
world. It comforts me more and more to realize and to observe and to feel
the great self-restoring power that the creatures in nature have while we human beings are making such a mess of things. . . . [P]oetry could remind
us of the need for restoration through inner nature. Also, I think that in the
poetry of nature there is the willingness to approach the living creatures with
a kind of attentiveness that is almost reverence.[4]

Until the "New Poems," Wright's reverence for nature had been apparent in his descriptive images, but his characteristic attitude had
been despair that human beings have so alienated ourselves from nature that we cannot participate fully in its healing powers. He now
develops a progressive sense that, although we have betrayed nature
in our human rapacity, we may yet achieve a limited harmony with
this source of healing. While he does not profess the optimism of the
romantics in nature's ability to heal man, he balances his concern for
our exploitation with confidence that a proper reverence for nature can
restore some health to humanity.

In *Shall We Gather at the River,* nature's creatures are victims of humanity. The "black Ohioan swan" of "Three Sentences for a Dead
Swan" was the victim of a polluted river, and the poet is not confident in his hope for the swan's resurrection. Another bird, "The
Small Blue Heron," as it croaks with terror, reminds the poet of a
casualty in a Nazi concentration camp who faced his certain death
with absurd dignity, asking the gatherer of bodies to place his on the
top of the pile because he has asthma. Neither the heron nor the man
of whom the heron reminds the poet is "the last one." The creature's
terror suggests to the poet that indifference to life by others is indeed
the condition human beings share with nature.

This attitude is modified in one of the more experimental "New
Poems," "A Secret Gratitude." The structure of this poem blends
Wright's meditation on the great love of the poet Edna St. Vincent
Millay and the Dutch importer Eugen Boissevain, with a memory of

an incident in which Wright and three companions resisted the impulse to harm five deer they encountered. Wright admires the depth of Boissevain's love for the bohemian poet, but wonders whether this constancy can be reconciled with the behavior of most people: "Was he human? I doubt it, / From what I know / Of men" (*CP*, 186).

What Wright knows of men in this particular poem combines a reverence for nature and contempt for human beings reminiscent of Jeffers's inhumanist philosophy. Wright condemns human beings as "chemical accidents of horror pausing / Between one suicide or another," and as creatures "capable of anything" with rhetoric that is at least as vitriolic as anything in Jeffers or Swift:

> Man's heart is the rotten yolk of a blacksnake egg
> Corroding, as it is just born, in a pile of dead
> Horse dung.
> I have no use for the human creature.
> He subtly extracts pain awake in his own kind.
> I am born one, out of an accidental hump of chemistry.
> I have no use.
>
> (*CP*, 185)

Taken by itself, this rhetoric seems self-indulgently cynical and quite inconsistent with the tone of Wright's poems. As elements in a rhetorical strategy, these sentiments contrast with the actual content of the poem, both Boissevain's love for Millay and the narrative of the encounter with the deer. Wright cannot explain, in light of this attitude, why he and his friends did not attempt to harm the deer. They had dogs to set upon them, and they could have escaped punishment "Because / Who cares?" (*CP*, 185), but they did not. That is one of the secret gratitudes of the title. If they were brutally inclined, they did not act on that inclination.

The other gratitude is his knowledge of Boissevain's love. Wright realizes that Millay's capacity, as a poet, to transform herself and reality contributed to that constancy: "Think of that. Being alive with a girl / Who could turn into a laurel tree / Whenever she felt like it" (*CP*, 186). More than an allusion to Daphne, who was turned into a laurel tree to escape an unwanted lover, this suggests the power of the creative imagination to transform the self through an act of will, as well as a synthesis of the volitional human spirit and the natural vitality of creation. That Wright intends a meaning like this one is clear from the final section, in which he "can hear a small waterfall rippling antiphonally down over / The stones of my poem" (*CP*,

186). If Wright cannot share Eugen's generosity of spirit or Edna's miracle of transformation, he can listen to nature as it chants in response to his own imaginative creation.

The regenerative power of nature helps the poet accept the universal fate of dying and being forgotten in "Eclogue at Nash's Grove." The primary element Wright retains from the traditional eclogue is the soliloquy about mutability, but he emphasizes the growth of the trees and flowers to obliterate the toil and economic striving that once went on in this grove. Representative of many similar scenes in our country, this now looks like "Virgin America, all right," despite the worn tombstones a close inspection discloses. Wright suspects that this beautiful scene has its own history of labor and economic rapacity: "No doubt the name belonged to some soft-eyed, sympathetic / Son of a bitch banker who stamped a Norwegian / Out of his money, this green place" (CP, 195). The green place has been restored by time, and Wright now wishes for a fitting elegy for the farmers who once owned it, for "Nash, whether he was a land gouger / Or not," for his own sons who are sometimes as unhappy as their father, for "the lives who are eaten away / By the plump rats of brief years," "And for me." Accepting the passage of time and perceiving the regeneration and forgiveness of nature, Wright wishes that his modern eclogue, like the grove itself, can become "a little / Darkness for them, where they do not have to weep. / Not for me, anyway" (CP, 196).

The last of the "New Poems," "Northern Pike," completes the design of coming to know and participate in the healing power of nature. Employing a strategy similar to that of "A Blessing" and "A Fishing Song" in *This Journey,* this poem affirms the joy of communion with nature in spite of hostile conditions. As the final poem in *Collected Poems,* it begins with an urgent thesis to affirm in the face of the many despairing texts in the collection: "All right. Try this, / Then." What is tried, however, seems to be a text for further despair:

> Every body
> I know and care for,
> And every body
> Else is going
> To die in a loneliness
> I can't imagine and a pain
> I don't know.
>   (CP, 213)

Only the most alert reader will see the small hope in this pessimistic prediction. Wright spaces between *every* and *body* to suggest that only the body will die. The poem is, however, about the needs of the body rather than the soul. It tells of catching and eating fish to sustain life, thus to participate in the cycle of predators that is our world. The finer instinct teaches generosity: "I would just as soon we let / The living go on living" (*CP,* 213). Survival takes precedence over intellect, but to reconcile the need of body with soul, the fishermen pray for muskrats, a policeman, and the blindness of the game warden, while they eat the fish.

The ultimate mood of the poem is not regret, but celebration: "There must be something very beautiful in my body, / I am so happy" (*CP,* 214). The poem sang of the beauty of the fish, and the accommodation of the needs of the body has been transformed into a genuine communion with nature. Wright's final word on our relation with nature, in *Collected Poems* at least, is that it rewards and forgives us as we participate in its processes.

Responsibility for the Past

Although many of Wright's poems deal with accepting the consequences of one's personal past, some treat taking responsibility for the sins and errors of the entire culture. American treatment of the Indian population was on Wright's mind as early as "Stages on a Journey Westward," and Indians in Minneapolis are often presented as inheritors of a legacy of indifference or brutality. In the "New Poems" "Red Jacket's Grave" and "A Centenary Ode: Inscribed to Little Crow, Leader of the Sioux Rebellion in Minnesota, 1862," his compassion for the state to which the white majority has driven the Indians leads to an acceptance of his personal responsibility in that process.

In the ode, Wright struggles to absolve himself from responsibility for the massacre of the Sioux more than a century ago: "I had nothing to do with it. I was not here. / I was not born" (*CP,* 180). His personal ancestors also "had nothing to do with it," because while Little Crow rebelled and was killed, his family was involved in a different rebellion. Some fought with the Confederacy, others with the Union, in another conflict that pitted American against American. Yet Wright cannot finally convince himself that this redeems them, and him, from guilt for the past: "it was not my fathers / Who murdered you. / Not much" (*CP,* 180).

Unable to ignore his responsibility in the death of the "true

father / Of my dark America," Wright recognizes the fragility of political loyalties, for his ancestors might have "run like hell from" the
Indians, or they might have joined them and run from the Confederacy or the Union. These impossible military allegiances turn love
among human beings into wrath, and cut the present off from even
the consolation of grief: "If only I knew where to mourn you, / I
would surely mourn" (CP, 181). Cut off from the ancestors who
fought and died in political struggles that now seem arbitrary, "The
hobo jungles of America grow wild again." Only death reconciles the
literal ancestors, "singing drunks and good carpenters," with the
figurative ancestor who defied the white majority. Their loyalties have
become insignificant, but Wright acknowledges that he must take responsibility for the past genocide that made possible the culture we
share.

Not only must we accept responsibility for the cruelties of the past,
whether or not we had a part in them, we must also be responsible
for the barbarities of our own time. This is the concern of one of
Wright's rare dramatic monologues, "A Mad Song for William S.
Carpenter, 1966." Wright's note indicates that Carpenter called a na-
palm strike against his own troops in Vietnam to prevent their surrender, then was decorated for bravery.

Wright tries to understand this conduct in a man who can quote
Catullus and who knows what hendecasyllabics are, and he comes up
with a surprisingly sympathetic account. As quarterback of his football team, Carpenter learned to sacrifice personal safety to achieve victory. He remembers throwing a touchdown pass while being knocked
unconscious. Now an officer, he is quarterback of another team,
where "terrified young men / . . . Lob one another's skulls
across / Wings of strange birds that are burning / Themselves alive"
(CP, 177). In the madness that was Vietnam, Carpenter applied to
the battlefield the lesson of American athletics, that winning is worth
any sacrifice. He was responsible for risking the lives of his soldiers.
But he was rewarded, and our entire culture made him the man he
was.

Accepting personal responsibility for the errors of our culture was
as hard for James Wright as it is for any of us. It was a necessary step
in his revised perspective on American experience in general, the
topic that organizes Two Citizens.

Chapter Five
"My Ohioan": *Two Citizens*

While honors for *Collected Poems* culminated with the Pulitzer Prize, Wright was at work devising new strategies for expression. In the "New Poems" he had complained about feeling dissatisfied with his accomplishment. As the collection brought fame to the poet, he followed the line of thought announced in "Many of Our Waters" and strove to find his own language in order to achieve his goal—writing the "poetry of a grown man."

Resisting the temptation to repeat the formulas that had succeeded so well in *Shall We Gather at the River* and *The Branch Will Not Break,* Wright continued to experiment with the more radically open forms he had attempted in the "New Poems." When he tried to press to its limit his aesthetic, the "pure clear word," the poems became uneven and more obscure than those in the major volumes. Striving for complete lucidity of expression, Wright lost some of the subtlety and refinement of feeling on which the success of the earlier poems had depended.

Wright was fully aware of the price he paid for clarity. He often condemned *Two Citizens* as his worst volume of poems, and in one interview declared with characteristic hyperbole that he would never write another book: "I've never written any book I've detested so much. No matter what anybody thinks about it, I know this book is final." After he had in fact published finer books, Wright modified, but did not repudiate, his judgment of the volume: "The book is just a bust. I will never reprint it. . . . It seems to me a bad book because most of it is badly written. Obscure and self-indulgent, it talks around subjects rather than coming to terms with them. It is impossibly ragged. It is just unfinished."[1] Although Wright never came to accept this volume as he eventually did *Saint Judas,* the poems represent an important step in his artistic growth.

Two Citizens confronts the sympathetic reader with many contradictions. It aims at complete lucidity, but contains more obscure phrases than any of the previous books, like the specialized language of "Emerson Buchanan," in which names like Franklin Pierce and Publius

Vergilius Maro are tested for scansion and the transformation of Buchanan into death and silence is described as his becoming "one half-
hendacasyllabic" and "almost an amphibrach." Ordinary words like
lonely, lovely, dark, and *beautiful,* that have taken on special resonances
in Wright's work now become automatic, and the sentiments they
imply are often vague. The crudity of American speech, which played
a minor role in *Shall We Gather* and "New Poems," vies with erudite
diction in the poems, and often sounds hollow, as in the curse that
ends "Ohio Valley Swains":

> You thought that was funny, didn't you, to mock a girl?
> I loved her only in my dreams,
> But my dreams meant something
> And so did she,
> You son of a bitch,
> And if I ever see you again, so help me in the sight of God,
> I'll kill you.[2]

It is not the crudity of the language, but that of the sentiment, that
rings false. The adolescent name-calling could conceivably be attrib-
uted to the poet's recovering his childhood rage at his inability to
stop the harassment of the girl, even though several years have inter-
vened. But the idle threat to kill someone, a baser emotion than the
rage of the language, has an element of posing about it. Wright's
poems advocate respect for the sanctity of all life, and the hyperbolic
threat to kill an enemy from the past, while it communicates sincere
frustration at the poet's inability to intervene successfully, does not
transform memory into poetic insight. Even more disturbing, on reflection, is the suggestion in the syntax, that the girl who was victimized means less than the poet's dreams.[3]

Most attempts to explain the unresolved tensions in *Two Citizens*
focus on the lengthy epigraph from Hemingway's "The Killers," a
typical example of the tough American speech Hemingway and his
followers, especially James M. Cain and Dashiell Hammett, developed as a literary style. Wright's allegiance has shifted from the somber tones of Hardy, the controlled pessimism of Robinson, or the
studied ambiguity of Frost, to the stoic, macho attitudes and rhetoric
of the tough guy writers. Williamson argues that this is a second watershed in Wright's stylistic development. Rhetoric becomes more
important than imagery, and the volume initiates a poetry of exaggeration, expletive, and extreme and fluctuating emotional stances. He

concludes that much of the rhetoric of *Two Citizens* is "cultural," an "emotional sound barrier" through which American males must break in order to achieve tenderness, when they have been taught to need and respect toughness. Smith evaluates the new style as a "halting, stammering movement whose function is to mediate between horror and tenderness." Costello holds that two distinct authorities now compete for the voice of Jenny, the muse of *Shall We Gather at the River* who here appears in "October Ghosts" and "Son of Judas," and concludes that Wright is unable to mediate successfully between the authority of Hemingway and that of Horace.[4]

The spirit of Horace is often felt in this collection. The popular title of one of his epistles, "Ars Poetica," is appropriated ironically for the first poem, and his spirit is addressed in "Prayer to the Good Poet." Wright always associated Horace with decorum and refinement. In "Ars Poetica," Horace advised young poets to be patient and deliberate, and Wright considered himself a classical poet. Wright's innate tendency toward spontaneity, combined with the Hemingway aesthetic of revising to achieve the effect of terse, elliptic conversation, often came into irreconcilable conflict with the refinement Horace advocated. When Wright was able to control the tensions among these influences, however, the writing was sure and powerful.

The mode of prayer central to *Shall We Gather* dominates "Prayer to the Good Poet" and many poems in this collection as well. Wright petitions Horace, his literary mentor, to teach him how to love his own father, a lifelong factory worker. Still coming to terms with his father's impending death, as in "Two Postures Beside a Fire," Wright emphasizes Dudley's superiority to the prejudices of his culture. While other workers "said dagoes," the elder Wright still tells his son he loves Italians. Wright synthesizes his own roots in literary and proletarian cultures through simple but effective wordplay:

> I worked once in the factory that he worked in.
> Now I work in the factory that you live in.
> Some people think poetry is easy,
> But you two didn't.
>
> (*TC*, 11)

Rather than distinguishing between the high culture of art and the low culture of manufacturing, Wright recognizes that all labor is productive, honorable, and demanding.

As Horace nurtured Wright's literary striving with classical rules and examples, Dudley nurtured him with love. These gifts made possible the person Wright has become and the legacy he can pass on to his son, now himself a poet. The poem seeks a calm resolution of the many selves that make up one man, a recognition of the sameness in differing occupations and regional inheritances and the comfort that comes from knowing that apparently conflicting elements in one's own identity can be mutually supportive.

Like most of the "New Poems," many in *Two Citizens* employ a structure that allows for the incorporation of diverse elements; and as rigidly formed a work as "Prayer to the Good Poet" has room for varied moods. One motif, heightening the contrast between the factory and the poet's study, is athletics as emblem for an excellence Wright does not consistently find in his America. With what must be an exaggeration characteristic of this book, Wright makes his father a figure of mythic proportions when he says Dudley, a Sunday baseball pitcher, once switched to left hand and struck out three batters. Another athlete, Bennie Capaletti, becomes a model for the restraint and decency Wright's two fathers embody, when he resists the temptation to slug someone who called him a "dirty guinea" during a basketball game, and Wright offers to Horace Bennie's restraint as a tribute to the decency of which some Americans are capable.

The international theme of bringing the Ohio to join with the Tiber as the river at which we must gather is the central concern toward which the diverse energies of *Two Citizens* are directed. Wright stated these intentions in a comment for the dust jacket. *"Two Citizens* is an expression of my patriotism, of my love and discovery of my native place. I never knew or loved my America so well, and I began the book with a savage attack upon it. Then I discovered it. It took the shape of a beautiful woman who loved me and who led me through France and Italy. That is why it is most of all a book of love poems. The two citizens are Annie and I." That Wright felt compelled to speak in such detail about his intentions suggests that he was not confident about this collection. The certainty that the order of the poems would make clear his intention, as had occurred in *The Branch* and *Shall We Gather,* failed the poet, and he wanted his readers to understand the collection's design. In an interview, he expanded his intentions in uncharacteristic detail: "we [he and Anne] know that we also love America. We know that at this time Americans, who are a good people and a kind of lost people, are suffering very badly. There is so much vitality in this country, there are so many good men, good, kind, intelligent men. Where did it all go wrong?"[5] Perhaps Wright knew that the poems of outrage would overwhelm those of reconciliation and that the arrangement of the poems would do little to counterbalance that impression.

Ohio, from Europe

With this perplexing and sometimes contradictory book, Wright's Ohio basin became the setting of a regional myth, in the manner of Hardy's Wessex, Joyce's Dublin, or Faulkner's Yoknapatawpha County. The idiosyncratic characters who populate the Martins Ferry region suffer dreary lives, punctuated by occasional moments of joy. Had Wright chosen fiction as his primary medium, he might have written a body of work comparable with that of these masters, but his poems provide crisp glimpses into the lives and manners of his native region. A closer prototype can be found in Robinson's Tilbury Town.

Although the professed intention of *Two Citizens* is to communicate Wright's reconciliation with his native land, seen from the new perspective of Europe, a rhetoric of indignation dominates the collection. The arrangement of the poems does not lead the reader inevitably to discover the love Wright professes in the dust jacket note, for the treatments of cherished memories, "Paul" and "The Old WPA Swimming Pool in Martins Ferry, Ohio," occur near the middle. Toward the end, "Emerson Buchanan" and "October Ghosts" develop incomplete and frustrated attempts to link up with that environment. If the arrangement does not lead us to the conclusion the poet advocates, perhaps a more subjective aesthetic judgment will do so. The poems about cherished memories, while less technically spectacular than those of indignation, are more permanently rewarding.

Despite being marred by its hyperbolic conclusion, "Ohio Valley Swains" is a brilliant cryptic narrative about human cruelty and indifference. Wright presents terse scenes from a memory, or more likely a composite memory, of the violation of a local girl by a gang of young thugs. The poem is organized around variations on the phrase, "here comes Johnny Gumball," the leader whose approach brings terror to the innocent. The narrative is punctuated by expletives that communicate both the vernacular of the Ohio gangs and the rage Wright feels that the crime was neither prevented nor punished. The

final curse may be described as Wright's futile attempt to punish a
wrong no one would deal with when it happened.

Against the tough guy vernacular of the narrative and the curse,
like the judgment "Guido don't give a diddly damn" when young
Wright approaches him to help Lilly—his name inevitably reminds
us of Dante's evil counsellor in Eliot's epigraph for "Prufrock"—
Wright balances two linguistic elements, an exerpt from the hymn
"Oh God Our Help in Ages Past" and the archaism *swains,* the ironic
resonance of which might be lost on someone unfamiliar with the
conventions of pastoral romance. Wright's blend of cryptic, fragmented narrative, allusion, and contrasting levels of diction suggests
the poetics of Eliot rather than the styles of Wright's principal collections.

This style serves Wright well in constructing his emblematic account of human cruelty and indifference. Obvious menaces to society,
Gumball's bullies once beat up Wright's brother, and Lilly, who cannot defend herself, has only a young boy as her champion; the thugs
"knocked me down" with ease. The youth appeals to a cross section of
society for help, but meets indifference everywhere. Guido is openly
indifferent and later joins the rapists in laughing about their deed.
Less obvious are the indifferent reactions of fundamentalist religion
and private authority.

While he searches for help, the boy passes a revivalist meeting. The
hymn being sung by "the insane Jesus Jumpers" (*TC,* 19) appeals to
God for help in the past and future, but the boy does not go there
for help. He knows that these people are too busy trusting in God
and speaking in "blind tongues" to take action in the present (the
only tense absent in the excerpt from their hymn) to prevent a vicious
attack on human dignity. The most effective counterpoint of the
poem is the laughter of the thugs just outside the revivalists' tent.
"Very politely" challenged by a railroad detective, the boy appeals to
him to help Lilly, but this authority, trained in physical violence,
tells him to go home. If it does not affect the railroad, what happens
to Lilly does not matter.

In this nightmarish adaptation of the parable of the Good Samaritan, Ohio is a hell of human cruelty and indifference. The child could
not save the girl, and no one else would. Although this does not justify the merely rhetorical curse at the end—for by this account the
enemy is not thugs but an indifferent society that will do nothing to
prevent their cruelty—the lapse in poetic judgment is understand-
able.

If Wright is an ineffectual champion of the oppressed in "Swains," he implicates himself in the rapacious attitudes that represent America at its worst in "Son of Judas," a title he also briefly considered for the collection. He had treated Judas as existential protagonist in "Saint Judas" and remembered "my poor Judas" as a broken man in "The Idea of the Good," but the poet now identifies with the traditional Judas who bargained his Master for silver. In a poem that has been called a "Blakean critique of the possibilities of good and evil in a society that presents no counterforce, political or religious, to acquisitive greed,"[6] Wright represents his choice between allegiances as two forms of aberrant sexual behavior.

Employing a Daphne allusion like the one in "A Secret Gratitude," Wright figures a moment when he discovered his love for nature as making "my secret love to" a sycamore tree. We soon discover that the "Jenny sycamore"—an obvious reference to the muse of the previous collection—is dead, so the transcendence of the material body the speaker found in this episode cannot be recovered. It was not a permanent alteration, for "when I came back down into my own body / Some Hanna among the angels / Strip-mined it" (*TC*, 8).

Hanna, an entrepreneur who influenced American politics at the turn of the century, is one of the angels of hell, but the poet is in no position to "damn Mark Hanna or anyone else" because he has succumbed to Hanna's materialism. The contrasting sexual metaphor, onanism, indicts Hanna's greed crudely and cynically:

> I was perfectly willing to accept your world,
> Where Mark Hanna and every other plant
> Gatherer of the grain and gouging son
> Of a God whonks his doodle in the
> United States Government of his hand.
>
> (*TC*, 8)

Masturbation represents exploitation of natural resources for the sake of profit, with the reciprocal benefit of being protected by and controlling the political system. Like onanism, this is a closed system, and the poet condemns himself for using his art to acquire money and fame: "I have bought your world. / I don't want it. / And I don't want all your money / I got sucked into making / Either" (*TC*, 9). As is often the case in diagnostic poetry, Wright is more persuasive in condemning materialism than in finding a way to resist it.

The polemical title "I Wish I May Never Hear of the United States Again" announces Wright's most defiantly exaggerated attitude, but the poem introduces a theme that unifies his criticism of the American experience. We have abused our language until it is no longer an instrument for effective communication or clear thinking. The title conditions us to expect more invective, but the poem is actually an account of Wright's learning a foreign language. In Yugoslavia, learning new words for greeting, farewell, mountain, cathedral and cheese, he discovers that these ideas become vital for him through the words he must master to name them. The title, then, has a double meaning: he rejects the corruption of language that has dulled and confused our appropriation of reality, and he wishes he could learn new words for the United States in order to recover the vitality that has been corrupted by our abuse of these words.

To invigorate our perception by learning new words is an appealing fantasy, but Wright is a realist who says in the final poem, "No, I ain't much. / The only tongue I can write in / Is my Ohioan" (*TC,* 58). The poet's task is to bring renewed vitality to our language, and Wright's invective is a barrier through which he must break to recover our language from the corruptions of politics and slogans. He was concerned with this corruption of language for the rest of his life. In an interview published a year before *Two Citizens,* he said, "It seems that all of our great ethical ideals always come to grief because, at least in part, our public figures take our language away from us, erode its meaning, so that we can't tell whether or not to trust other people when they make some public gesture in language. We're left sort of scrambling around in the dark, trying to help one another, and yet, being afraid to." In that and a subsequent interview, he names several prominent officials as examples of subverting the function of language, but he prefaces the later remarks with, "I really do believe that there is, in language, something like a power to heal itself, to right itself."[7] One obligation of poets is to participate in that healing process.

This sentiment is central to the scathing attack with which Wright opens the volume, "Ars Poetica: Some Recent Criticism." This anecdote about Aunt Agnes and Uncle Sherman is really an attempt to come to terms with the poet's loss of faith in his native land. Three times he varies the lines, "When I was a boy, / I loved my country," implying that uncritical patriotism is juvenile. One source of his disillusionment is the debasement of language, as he exhorts us in the philosophical climax: "Reader, / We had a lovely language, / We would not listen" (*TC,* 6). If his childhood love for the country has deteriorated because of disillusionment, the abused language has lost its vitality through neglect. In the final section Wright includes two lines in Latin to show what happens to a language that loses its vitality as an instrument for communication.

Although less experimental than "Ohio Valley Swains," this narrative is a cryptic account of the love Aunt Agnes gave and received. In this way, the poem provides a counterpoint for the love between James and Anne, the other main subject of the volume. This association is explicit: "I too have fallen in / With a luminous woman" (*TC,* 3). "Luminous" applies ironically to Aunt Agnes. She was homely, she and her house "stank," she did only one intelligent thing in her life (losing her temper when Uncle Emerson insulted her at her wedding), and when the poem was written she was in an insane asylum in Cambridge, Ohio. Yet for all her misfortunes, she was loved,[8] and that is one of the mysteries of "Ars Poetica." Uncle Sherman "must have been / One of the heroes / Of love," but the poet too wants to gather Agnes, with all her faults, "into my veins." The central anecdote answers the cynical question, "Why do I care for her, / That slob, / So fat and stupid?" (*TC,* 5).

Once Agnes performed an instinctive act of charity. A runaway goat turned into her alley, which Wright calls "my country, / If you haven't noticed," and the poem becomes a moral parable. Lacking the judgment to make an ethical decision, Agnes impulsively did the right thing: she "Threw stones back at the boys / And gathered the goat, / Nuts as she was, / Into her sloppy arms" (*TC,* 6). Pathetic and funny as this is, in this volume it is a unique act of kindness from Wright's youth.

The main point of the poem is that Wright has lost the innocence even to believe wholeheartedly in this experience:

> I don't believe in your god.
> I don't believe my aunt Agnes is a saint.
> I don't believe the little boys
> Who stoned the poor
> Son of a bitch goat
> Are charming Tom Sawyers.
>
> (*TC,* 6)

This series of disbeliefs covers some of our most cherished religious and cultural myths, such as the benevolent mischief of children.[9]

Wright has become so disillusioned that he no longer trusts even simple facts: "I don't believe in the goat either." Deprived of the myths
of his past, and unable to believe in new ones to replace them, all he
has left is outrage, so the poem ends with the open-ended curse that
characterizes so many of the criticisms of Ohio: "Hell, I ain't got
nothing. / Ah, you bastards, . . . / How I hate you" (*TC*, 7). A simplistic reading would identify the "bastards" as the boys who harassed
the goat, but that curse would be as empty as the one that ends
"Swains." It is more likely that the epithet refers to those who have
corrupted the language until we can no longer listen and to those
whose conduct has so disillusioned the poet that he doubts even the
positive value of the automatic gesture of his insane aunt.

Agnes almost becomes a positive emblem, but Jenny, whom the
prayer "October Ghosts" addresses, is no longer the flawed muse of
"Speak" and "To the Muse." She is now the "fat blossoming grand-
mother of the dead," and Wright addresses her as "Jenny darkness,
Jenny cold" (*TC*, 55). She has become a goddess of death, and
Wright appeals to her to help him make his peace with his own October, the disappointment of his expectatons. Preparing to become
himself a ghost, to walk with Jenny and Callimachus "Into the
gorges / Of Ohio, where the miners / Are dead with us" (*TC*, 54),
the speaker recalls a few relationships from youth when he sought,
but could not find, Jenny. The prayer becomes an elegy of acceptance
for the passing of all things: "We came so early, we thought to stay
so long. / But it is already midnight, and we are gone" (*TC*, 55).
This acceptance of death makes up some of Wright's most beautiful
lines. Immediately, he acknowledges debts to Robinson, to Jenny, to
nature and beauty. Yet the poem ends with a resignation unusual in
even an elegy: "Now I know nothing, I can die alone" (*TC*, 55). Having thought his way back to innocence, Wright is able to accept the
alienation with which so many of his poems have contended.

Two companion poems near the center of the collection express
Wright's reconciliation with his Ohio, and both vary the theme of
"Ars Poetica": the unexpected blessing that finally qualifies his condemnation of America. Both are among the finest in the book, but
each is an account of an exceptional, not a common, experience.

The style influenced by Hemingway is entirely appropriate for
"Paul," a brief narrative about a poor but skilled truck driver who
befriended the unhappy youth. Already having an intuition that Martins Ferry was a cultural waste land, the boy "had a pretty good
idea / It was hell. / What else are you going to get / When you ain't

got nothing?" (*TC,* 24). Paul's kindness gives the poet one ethical point of reference in the labyrinth of middle America: "If I care for anything, I care / For the man who picked me up on the street" (*TC,* 24). Paul becomes Wright's emblem for the self-reliant, honorable man who "can stand up in the middle of America / (That brutal and savage place whom I still love)" (*TC,* 25).

Yet in this tribute, Wright must acknowledge that he and Paul can no longer communicate, because the poet has chosen to labor in the factory of the intellect. Describing Paul's expertise as a driver, Wright alludes to Alceus's love for Sappho, and this pulls him up short: "You wouldn't even know what I'm talking about." As he realizes that his range of reference is more erudite than Paul's, he confronts a sterner truth, that he would no longer understand Paul, either. Despite the awareness that they would have difficulty in communicating, Wright intends this poem to salute an individual heroic act of kindness unusual in his America.

If individual merit motivates gratitude in "Paul," a creative ritual by the community is celebrated in "The Old WPA Swimming Pool in Martins Ferry, Ohio." Many of Wright's now mythic relatives responded to the collective intuition that the "river, / That is supported to be some holiness, / Starts dying" (*TC,* 22) by digging a swimming pool for their families. This life-giving substitute for the dying river was a welcome contrast to the other man-made holes the boy had seen in earth, "And you know what they were."

When these "fierce husbands" and "good men" combined their energies to create an alternative to the polluted river, they achieved a minor miracle, and it becomes the location of other miracles as well:

> Oh never mind, Jesus Christ, my father
> And my uncles dug a hole in the ground,
> No grave for once. It is going to be hard
> For you to believe: when I rose from that water,
>
> A little girl who belonged to somebody else,
> A face thin and haunted appeared
> Over my left shoulder, and whispered, Take care now,
> Be patient, and live.
>
> > > (*TC,* 23).

Although the girl's phrase is anachronistic, belonging to the Vietnam, not Depression, era, her message is quintessential Wright. Patience is the virtue that survives the despair of "The Idea of the

Good," and choosing life in the face of all its hazards is the single dominant theme of Wright's work. This message from the water nymph and human urchin gives the poet his equipment for living, something to balance against the harsh claims of Jenny. The reference to Jesus Christ is not a curse here, but an apostrophe that recognizes that the disinterested love central to Christian teaching is possible in middle America.

A few poems in *Two Citizens* use humor to take the edge off the negative judgments of America. The morbid joke of a telephone call to the dead, recalling the third chapter of Joyce's *Ulysses,* ends the poet's effort to communicate with his lost ancestors in "Emerson Buchanan." The tourist's habit of leaving a mark, often initials, on landmarks is satirized in "Names Scarred at the Entrance to Chartres," but the poet grudgingly accepts his community with P. Dolan and A. Doyle, the "two vulgars" with whom he must enter the cathedral. While deploring their lack of taste, Wright must acknowledge his shared inheritance with the arrogant American tourists. An imaginative variation on the convention of looking at our culture through the eyes of an anthropologist from another planet, "To You, Out There (Mars? Jupiter?)" advises the stranger that "You will not find God" here, but "you" will find incomprehensible customs like standing in line "To pray to someone whose name / Is Streisand" (*TC,* 42).

This humor, combined with the recollection of generous and life-giving labors by his uncles and Paul, helped Wright to balance his outrage at how far short of our potential we Americans have fallen. To reconcile himself with life in general would require the counterweight of the collection, the love poems. As *Shall We Gather at the River* explored the relation between physical and spiritual love, the love James felt for Anne in Europe inspired him to overcome his wrath at America. If it is an attack on America by a loving expatriate, *Two Citizens* is also a record of Anne's displacing Jenny as Wright's muse.

Love Poems

One distinctive feature of James Wright's personality was that he was always surprised to discover that he was loved. This discovery restored his sense of self-worth and gave him confidence to continue with his work. Although this is by no means a unique need, Wright was a poet, and one thing a poet does is to give expression to universal feelings. From the first, Wright was a love poet, but most of the love poems before *Two Citizens* were really laments about the transiency, fragility, or frustrations of love. In *Shall We Gather at the River,* he began to explore the relation between the love of the senses and that of the spirit. That collection was, however, dominated by the bitter muse Jenny, who became in the poetry not only a trader in love, a prostitute, but also a symbol for unapproachable and irreconcilable love. Perhaps the placement of "October Ghosts" near the end of the collection is Wright's attempt to put her ghost behind him by recognizing her as the goddess of death. Jenny never again appeared as an important figure in his work.

His second marriage brought order and focus to the poet's troubled personal life. In his many public comments on *Two Citizens* he insisted that his wife Anne was the inspiration who helped him come to terms with his outrage at the disappointment of his expectations for America. In their rediscovery of America from the shores of Europe, Wright also came to reevaluate the nature of love. He learned, and the love poems express, that love is not necessarily a risk of transiency and frustration, or an ideal dreamed about by poets of the past, but a simple, universal sharing of experience that can make our existential solitude a blessing rather than a curse.

We may take as a thesis for the love poems in *Two Citizens* the closing lines of "The Art of the Fugue: A Prayer," in which the poet offers those who pass his grave a legacy, the wisdom of his life: "Though love can be scarcely imaginable Hell, / By God, it is not a lie" (*TC,* 44). If love, what remains possible for human beings in the final analysis, cannot promise happiness, at least it promises truth.

The feeling that solitude is a blessing as well as a curse animates "Voices Between Waking and Sleeping in the Mountains." This poem carefully balances the claims of respect for the separate existence of the beloved against those of the sharing of experience we normally associate with love. Wright finds that it is no contradiction to assert both these claims at the same time: to love truly is to value the separateness of the other as a condition of really sharing a meaningful experience. This theme is communicated by means of a contrast between reason, here associated with waking, and the unconscious, here represented by a dream. While the poet's lover has taken a walk, to pursue an interest the poet cannot share with her, he accepts his separation with mild resentment. Using a metaphor drawn from "The Jewel," in *The Branch Will Not Break,* Wright considers his beloved's

soul one that has achieved wholeness, whereas he feels that his own
search will never end: "There is something in you that is able to discover the crystal. / Somewhere in me there is a crystal that I cannot
find / Alone" (*TC*, 35). His crystal, or his inescapable self, cannot be
disclosed because the poet is always burdened by thoughts of death.
His wife, having completed her essential self, pursues her calm search
for the "secret" she sees in the mountain snow. Yet there is something approaching pique in the insistence that the poet cannot find
his own essence alone, while his model for completeness has gone off
to find a secret that has nothing to do with him.

In this situation, the poet courts unconscious solitude in the form
of a dream. He falls asleep, and in his dream he seeks his own secret,
"something I was trying to find / In that dream" (*TC*, 35). His secret
discloses death and terror, for at the bottom of his dream is a nightmare, a savage Janus-figure who combines a face of cruelty and one of
death. It is tempting to speculate that this figure is Wright's river-
goddess of death, a combination of the harpy of "Humming a Tune
for an Old Lady in West Virginia" and the ubiquitous Jenny. As the
noose of the nightmare tightens with terror and despair, Wright cries
out in his sleep, and the voices between waking and sleeping help
him understand that real love is respect for the separateness of the
beloved.

In Eliot's "Prufrock" "human voices wake us, and we drown"; the
opposite occurs in this poem. The human voice, rescuing Wright
from his nightmare of solitude, enables him finally to approve it as
"my good dream," a quest into the unconscious relieved of its terror
by love. The poet is now able to understand the nature of solitude
and its role in love. This discovery of the fundamental relation between love and solitude is a source of freedom as well as a commitment to the future:

> Annie, it has taken me a long time to live.
> And to take a long time to live is to take a long time
> To understand that your life is your own life.
> What you found on that long rise of mountain in the snow
> Is your secret.
>
> (*TC*, 36)

To take so much time means to find out for ourselves that there is no
contradiction between the overwhelming need to be part of someone
else's existence and the reservation of that jewel that is our own sepa-

rate life. In keeping with this recognition, the poet shares with his beloved the memory of his first erotic and spiritual love for nature, probably the story of the same "Jenny sycamore" he recounted in "Son of Judas." Wright is unsure that he has the skill to share this memory fully with his wife, but a new confidence in the future balances the uncertainty about his communication: "Some day I may know how [to tell the story]" (*TC*, 36).

Wright ends the poem with a pledge to respect the secret his beloved found in the mountains: "I love your secret. By God I will never violate the wings / Of the snow you found rising in the wind. / Give them, keep them, love" (*TC*, 36). If the language is contemporary, the commitment is Elizabethan. A demand to share entirely the life of the beloved is to be in love merely with a mirror for one's self. To be in love is to charish those experiences that make the beloved a separate person, and this poem applies his belief in "minding one's own good business" even to lovers. To love a person is in fact to love the private experiences that make that person unique. Only by cherishing this privacy can one respect as well as love someone else.

"Afternoon and Evening at Ohrid" combines Wright's concern about the ability of language to limit our perceptions with his theme of the healing power of love. Vacationing in a small resort in southwestern Yugoslavia, the poet and his love try to compensate for their lack of knowledge of the proper words in Serbo-Croatian to give names to the beautiful flowers they find there. Wright effectively uses synaesthetic imagery to lament his inability to tell his love the correct name of "that small flower song." He articulates the loneliness of being unable to verbalize their relationship with the exciting new environment by mixing iambic and anapestic feet: "and so we had to keep / Our own words in the vastness of that place" (*TC*, 16).

Keeping our own words, however, requires strategies that may not do justice to their mutual perception. The beloved, already "grieved" by summer's end, is even more unhappy because she cannot give exact definition to the beauty around her, so the poet offers an embrace that is also a sharing of the alienation she feels: "That was all I had." Not entirely satisfied by this participation in her unhappiness, Wright attempts to use the stock in trade of the poet by constructing metaphors in his American English to compensate for their ignorance of Serbo-Croatian. Then the flower becomes a lover, and they share an artificial harmony with nature, in that its beauty reflects their affection. Wright employs the tough guy diction prominent in the collection to signify his dissatisfaction with falsifying an experience by exploiting metaphor to compensate for a lack of knowledge: "Well, / For the first time in my life, / I shut up and listened" (TC, 16).

When the metaphor ceases to satisfy, the poet attempts to understand what he listens to by creating an analogy. This device has the advantage of seeing relations between two distinct entities without blurring the distinctions. By this process, the unfamiliar can be understood in terms of the familiar. In order to understand the "silly love" the lovers feel for the unnamed flower, the poet wishes to encounter a familiar and beloved object, for "I already know / My friends the spiders" (TC, 17). Because he can evaluate his feelings about spiders in his native language, he can confidently propose a set of metaphors that link his feelings about these creatures with other beloved things. They can be "mountains," the landscape of Ohrid; or they can be women: "Every spider in America is the shadow / Of a beautiful woman" (TC, 17). Now that he is comfortably thinking in metaphors consistent with his own language and experience, Wright's perspective changes, and in the new "architecture / Of my eyes," he finds that the "best spider" at Ohrid communicates with a language that is neither Serbo-Croatian nor American. It is the language of feeling.

The poem is resolved not by linguistic strategy, but by discarding language and nominalism altogether. The beloved tells the poet to "Come to me and love me clearly with the thinning shadow of the turtle." This request introduces yet another metaphor, but one that leads back to intense feeling. Turtles combine reptilian skills for movement and survival on both land and water, and the metaphor suggests a love that can survive the end of summer and alienation from nature because of linguistic barriers. The poem concludes with an exchange that can only suggest transcendence of even language and names for these pure feelings that need not be named: "What is your name, / I said. / I love you, / She said" (TC, 17). Her being has been transformed to the love she feels, and further linguistic conveniences are not necessary.[10]

Stylistic experimentation marks "You and I Saw Hawks Exchanging the Prey," a poem that shows clear affinities with Whitman's "The Dalliance of the Eagles." Although Wright's subject matter is less explicit than Whitman's, the sharing of the field mouse captured by the male has implicit erotic signification, and the viewing by the human lovers causes this act to become a synonym for human love. Wright uses an unusually crisp form in this poem. Three stanzas are three lines long, two are a single line, and the remaining eight are two lines. Wright varies trimeter and dimeter lines, to give a sharp, imagistic focus in the manner of Williams.

Like Whitman, Wright emphasizes the parting of his birds of prey. Whitman ends with, "their separate diverse flight, / She hers, he his, pursuing," and Wright notes that the female falcon "flies away sorrowing. / Sorrowing, she goes alone" (*TC*, 50). Wright sees in the majesty and shared love of his hawks an emblem for the power of human love. It is fitting that this love poem, written by an American trying to come to grips with his disappointment at the failure of American ideals, was so profoundly influenced by the most thoroughly American poets of two centuries, Whitman and Williams.

A Composite Muse, "A Poem about Gold"

Although *Two Citizens* records the displacement of the dead Jenny by the living muse Anne Wright, in the most dazzling poem of the collection, Anne and Jenny are synthesized with many other muses, living, dead, and imagined. "Bologna: A Poem about Gold" is one of Wright's most impressive achievements. In it, Wright unifies his consistent preoccupations with art, nature, religion, politics, and love.

The composite muse is Mary Magdalene, as represented in Raphael's *St. Cecilia,* a large canvas housed in the Pinacoteca in Bologna. Wright imagines the painting as virtually coming to life, just as he treats Michelangelo's final Pieta as possessing animate character in "The Last Pieta, In Florence." In both poems, Wright concentrates the reader's attention on a peripheral figure in the work of art. His attention in "The Last Pieta" focuses on the old man, not the Holy Mother and Son, and in "Bologna" he calls our attention to Mary Magdalene, standing at the far right and looking out at the audience, while the other figures in the painting focus on the saint.

Wright chooses Mary over the more proper Saint Cecilia, whom he sees as overly self-absorbed, "Adoring / Herself" and "Smirking." His ambiguous phrase, "letting her silly pipes wilt down," accurately describes Raphael's portrait. The saint holds this instrument loosely, angled toward discarded musical instruments at her feet, while she looks upward toward a beatific vision. Mary, on the other hand, is portrayed by Wright as an earthy, forgiving, and hopeful figure:

> while the lowly and richest of all women eyes
> Me the beholder, with a knowing sympathy, her love
> For the golden body of the earth, she knows me,
> Her halo faintly askew,
> And no despair in her gold
> That drags thrones down
> And then makes them pay for it.
>
> (*TC,* 38)

Mary comes to life in the painting, because of her slight dishabille, her love for created things, her sympathy for the beholding poet, and her ability to topple mere politicians and dynasties. For Wright, she is the true creature of gold, the lover of earth and man, and the defier of human conventions.

The Biblical Mary Magdalene was a woman of mixed reputation. She was certainly the woman from whom Jesus "had cast seven devils" (Mark 16.9 and Luke 8.2), and she was probably the woman who washed the Master's feet while other followers questioned Jesus for allowing such a sinner to minister to him and were reprimanded: "her sins, which are many, are forgiven; for she loved much" (Luke 7.47). Many Biblical scholars believe Mary was a harlot, and this account of her past corresponds with Wright's many poems about prostitutes, from "Gesture by a Lady with an Assumed Name" to the Jenny poems. Forgiven her past, Mary Magdalene became a loyal follower of Jesus. She was among the last to leave the scene of the Crucifixion and one of the first to arrive at the empty tomb. In one account, she was the first person to whom the risen Christ appeared, and she recognized him upon hearing his voice. He instructed her to carry the message of the resurrection to the faithful (John 20.11–18). Wright's composite muse, then, is a sinner and lover of the earth, forgiven her indiscretions and rewarded by a divine responsibility.

Perhaps because of the religious tone of the painting, Wright defends his choice of the sinner over the saint. In this defense, he balances the claims of the morally pure and perhaps pharisaical against those of the artist. Mary may "look sorry" to Saint Cecilia and to the "right-hand saint on the tree," but

> She didn't look sorry to Raphael,
> And

> I bet she didn't look sorry to Jesus
> And
> She doesn't look sorry to me.
> (Who would?)
> She doesn't look sorry to me.
> (TC, 38–39)

Wright associates himself, by means of effective repetition and self-effacement, with the artist who saw and communicated the beauty of the earthy Mary and the Master who saw her beauty when others could not. Having made this choice, he associates the artist and the creator as those who embrace life rather than pass judgment on others.

In addition to Raphael, another artist is mentioned in "Bologna." This prayer contains an apostrophe to Horace, Wright's "first and severe / Italian," to whom "Prayer to the Good Poet" was addressed. Wright petitions Horace for the discipline and style to craft his poem to capture the radiance of Mary and the sunlight in which her continuing presence is manifest. Out of his appreciation for the painting of Raphael and the craft of Horace, Wright creates his own singular artistic construction. The poem has a unique organization, and it blends colloquial with poetic styles skillfully. More than most of his poems, this one uses repetition effectively.

The controlling symbol is the "White wine of Bologna," which is actually golden in color, and which connects the spiritual with the erotic, much as Mary's past and time with Jesus are connected. The wine, produced by the prolonged action of Mary's sun on the grapes of Bologna, is the vessel of communions both within and without the cathedral. When he mentions "the heavy wine in the old green body, / The glass that so many have drunk from" (TC, 38), Wright implies both the communion shared in cathedrals by the faithful over many centuries and the sexual union that, like communion, revitalizes the "old body" with the vitality suggested by the color green. In one of the several daring metaphors of the poem, Wright suggests that shared erotic love can enable us to come to the cathedral radiant with the health of holiness: "I have brought my bottle back home every day / To the cool cave, and come forth / Golden on the left corner / Of a cathedral's wing" (TC, 38). There is a death-rebirth suggestion in the emergence from the cave of the self,[11] but the poem emphasizes a radiance the communicant can bring to communion.

The third communion of "Bologna," that of the perceiver with the product of the creative artist, in this case Wright with Raphael, brings the poem to a splendid and optimistic conclusion. Reflecting on the artist's rendering of the earthy yet divine presence of Mary and her forgiving, embracing glance, Wright sees that this kind of blessing is available to all lovers who seek it. Extending the metaphor in which Bologna's wine serves as vehicle for the communions with earth, art, the divine, and the human, Wright finds that his divinity has been with him all along:

> Mary in Bologna, sunlight I gathered all morning
> And pressed in my hands all afternoon
> And drank all day with my golden-breasted
>
> Love in my arms.
>   (*TC*, 39)

In this metaphor, the lover is both producer and consumer of the vehicle for the greatest communion of all, the one that teaches us our essential unity with each other, nature, art, and God.

With this magnificent poem, in which he reassured himself of the validity of that fundamental truth that there is no contradiction between secular and divine love, Wright was able to put behind him the anger that had driven the early poems of *Two Citizens*. With that anger resolved, he was free to be the poet of hope he really wanted to be. This mature vision would be the substance of *To a Blossoming Pear Tree*.

Chapter Six
"The Inmost Secret of Light": The Final Volumes

Wright quickly repudiated *Two Citizens* because of its tendency toward overstatement and its unexamined judgments. Despite the obvious excellence of individual works like "Bologna: A Poem About Gold," the collection as a whole exhibits more sincerity than style, more anger than art. The political poems do not uniformly succeed in converting outrage into poetry, and the love poems often substitute vague sentiments for precise insight into the meaning of those feelings. Wright knew that he had pushed his conviction about the "pure clear word" beyond the limits inherent in that hypothesis, and that recognition accounts for his extreme disappointment with the volume.

To a Blossoming Pear Tree is superior to *Two Citizens,* because Wright comes to terms with his bitterness and adopts a tone of tolerance rather than condemnation. Combining the strategies of *Saint Judas* and *The Branch Will Not Break* enhanced by a renewed devotion to classical poetry, Wright exhibits a mature attitude. The subtle tones and shadings occur partly because he replaces the essentially rhetorical gifts of *Two Citizens* with more lyrical gifts in the new collection.

At the center of this tolerance and disciplined art is a renewed vision. From the first, Wright sympathized with the radical imperfection of individual human beings. What attracted him to Jenny, Harding, the lady with an assumed name, Minnegan Leonard, George Doty, and the vast number of outcasts in his poems was an understanding of their imperfection. In *To a Blossoming Pear Tree* and the other final volumes, Wright extends the principle of sympathy with the imperfect to human institutions as well as individuals. The rage of the "New Poems" and *Two Citizens* centered on the failure of our institutions to live up to their promise. Now, he realizes that America, or any human state, is an organic entity destined by its evolutionary nature to fall short of our highest expectations for it. This does not of course mean that we should accept that failure passively, and Wright's poems continue to criticize our public failures. What is at stake here is a shift in tone, one that harmonizes the poet's expressive role with the responsibility of the citizen.

The final volumes suggest that Wright overcame his penchant for overstatement and vituperation because he recognized that an institution or a culture cannot be a Platonic or even a Jeffersonian ideal maintained in its pure form. It is rather a dynamic contract that adapts itself to the demands of time and the personalities of its citizens and leaders. Each step in the adaptation will be traumatic and will produce errors. What Wright learned, after lashing out with the invective in *Two Citizens,* was that the most productive attitude toward an institution is a critical love-hate relationship based on, and ruled by, tolerance.

For poets and philosophers, disappointment and pain are sources of wisdom. For James Wright, the anger of the "New Poems" and *Two Citizens* led to the wisdom and tolerance that make possible the more subtle poetry of the final volumes. With *To a Blossoming Pear Tree,* he accomplished the goal he had set in "Many of Our Waters"—to write the "poetry of a grown man."

Prose Pieces

Among the pleasant surprises for readers of the final volumes are the fourteen prose entries in *To a Blossoming Pear Tree* and the eighteen in *This Journey.* Wright began to explore this form seriously shortly after completing *Two Citizens.* By 1976, he had published prose pieces in three major anthologies.[1] That year, he brought out a handsome limited edition of prose complemented by six of Joan Root's drawings. *Moments of the Italian Summer* contains only one poem, and it was written by Anne Wright. All of James's work is prose meditation. Several of these appear, often judiciously revised, in *To a Blossoming Pear Tree.*

It is tempting to speculate that collaboration with his son Franz in translating Hesse's *Wandering* contributed to Wright's decision to edit and revise his journal entries for publication. He had translated his own selection of thirty-one poems by Hesse two years earlier, but with *Wandering* he came to terms with the German writer in a freely meditative, loose structure that allows for the free play of imagination. If the form itself suggested a new set of possibilities, the emotional impact of collaborating with his son must have added to the pleasure associated with the prose meditation. Echoing the central feeling of poems like "Having Lost My Sons, I Confront the Wreckage of the Moon: Christmas, 1960," "The Last Drunk," in *Two Citizens,* records the anguish of prolonged estrangement from his first son: "I sired a bitter son. / I have no daughter" (*TC,* 12). Mrs. Wright explained in a private interview that Wright saw his own inner turmoil in Franz's personality. Working together to translate Hesse, the two poets moved closer to one another, and Wright lovingly understates their cooperation in his note to the book. He says he translated the prose, but credits his son with the poetry: "Then we helped each other." That this effort helped to resolve the conflict between the father and son is further suggested by a comment in *Moments of the Italian Summer* that may serve as a gloss on the intentions of all the prose poems. At the center of "A Letter to Franz Wright," the parent speaks of the implicit contract between writer and reader that governs reading the prose pieces:

There are these fragments of words I picked up on the hither side of my limits. I am sending them to you, because you will love them. Consequently, you will know how to piece them together into a vision of your own design. Your imagination is not mine. How could it be? Who would want it to be? I wouldn't. You wouldn't. But I love both, so I trust yours. Here are some fragments of my hammer that broke against a wall of jewels.[2]

Wright's trust that his son will reassemble the vision of the prose piece in his own imagination of course extends to the reader, but the appreciation of the otherness of the son's imagination adds emotional weight to the suspicion that their collaboration on Hesse's book had special psychological significance for the elder Wright.

If we cannot be sure what motivated Wright to make public his private meditations, we can be positive that he had long been concerned with the real difference between poetry and prose. More than a decade before the first dated prose piece, he had written in his afterword to Hardy's *Far from the Madding Crowd* an irritated dismissal of the controversy over distinguishing poetry from prose: "That discussion is physically depressing, like a stupid joke which everyone present has known and loathed for years. I should like to record my gratitude to Mr. Yvor Winters for his beautifully impatient statement that poetry is written in verse, whereas prose is written in prose."[3] While composing the pieces included in *Moments of the Italian*

Summer, he wrote an essay for *Field* magazine in which he tried to define the musical unit of a poetic line, as opposed to a prose cadence. In his final recorded interview, he concluded that, while there is a fundamental difference between the musical unit of a poetic line and the rhythm of prose, "I don't think that, in any deep sense, it makes a damn bit of difference whether or not one is writing in prose or in verse, just so he's trying to be imaginative and true to what he is hearing." In that interview, he confirmed that the prose grew from his journal entries. Still, he contended that "[i]ts rhythm and its music are different from that of my poems, really."[4]

Critical opinion and reader response have generally approved the choice Wright made. The majority opinion has been voiced by Yenser, who sees in Wright's use of the device a "tolerance for loose ends," an "appetite for disgression," and a "fugitive unity" that is very much in keeping with his attitudes expressed in more traditional poetic forms.[5] We have commented in previous chapters on Wright's desire to incorporate a variety of levels of experience within a single poem, especially in "New Poems" and *Two Citizens,* and the prose in the last two major volumes, while pointed and highly focused, allows him the expansiveness toward which he aimed his longer poems. One immediate effect of claiming the option to use prose for the more diverse subjects is that the traditional poems of *To a Blossoming Pear Tree* and *This Journey* are more tightly unified than those of the previous volume. In this respect, the final collections remind us of the best work in *The Branch Will Not Break.*

The prose adds variety to these books. It allows Wright a format for a meditative strategy to supplement that of his poems. In the best prose, he moves gracefully from a scene or a situation, through metaphor or related devices of association, to a meditation on his subject. This is the strategy of "The Fruits of the Season," in which a community exhibition of paintings, "the enduring fruits of five hundred years," contrasts with a marketplace full of literal "fruits of the season in a glory that will not last too long."[6] Wright does not pose a choice between the metaphoric fruits, the great art of the past, and the literal fruit condemned to brief glory then decay, but as he sees the analogy with human life implicit in the contrast, he comes to a peaceful acceptance of mortality with its transient glory: "But they [the literal fruits] will last long enough. . . . I have eaten the first fruit of the season, and I am in love" (*BPT,* 55). With remarkable dexterity, Wright has moved from literal imagery through metaphor to a reasoned acceptance of the transiency of living things.

An ideal representative of Wright's style as well as strategy in the prose piece is "A Lament for the Shadows in the Ditches." Typically, this meditation begins by emphasizing the physical setting of the writer much in the manner of a studied journal entry or a familiar essay. In setting the scene, Wright appeals to his readers' olfactory, visual, and tactile senses. The noontime sun is brilliant enough to hurt the eyes, and it must be hot. The cappuccino the poet sips appeals to our taste and smell, and even the sidewalk cafe table at which he sits is "wobbly." The literal scene also suggests memories of the poet's personal past, ranging from the beauty of the river, to the "black ditch of horror" in which a youth drowned, to streetcars—now merely a memory and ultimately a synecdoche for the entropy of life itself in the Ohio basin, "when everything in Ohio ran down and yet never quite stopped?" (*BPT,* 11).

The memory of the ditch as a place of disaster, and the association of Roman and American entropy, lead Wright to contemplate in imagination the nearby scene of willed disasters, the Colosseum, "an intricate and intelligent series of ditches" that the sun cannot reach. These images in turn yield a set of metaphors that suggest the ubiquity of cruelty in human history. The literal darkness of the ditches suggests "the shadows of starved people who did not even want to die." Now that the central metaphor has been established by a process very similar to free association, Wright speculates on the nature of martyrdom and the guilt that remains with all of us because human beings were suffered to die: "There is no way to get rid of the shadows of human beings who could find God only in that last welcome of the creation, the maws of tortured animals. Is that last best surest way to heaven the throat of the hungry?" (*BPT,* 11).

Rather than pursue this speculative crux, Wright turns to a related set of metaphors to evoke the beauty of beasts whose cruelty was exploited by those who wanted martyrs. The sunlight in the Colosseum becomes "the golden shadow of a starved lion," which in turn challenges Wright's beloved horses as the most beautiful of God's creatures. Wright has recaptured the strategy of many of the best poems in *The Branch Will Not Break* by moving from literal observation through memory and surreal imagery to a purely imaginative perception.

Quite similar to "Lament" in structure, but almost opposite in tone, is "The Secret of the Light." It also begins with subtle description. Wright sits "contented and alone" in a park in Verona "glimpsing the mists of early autumn as they shift and fade" to illuminate

natural beauty around the river. The diction conveys tranquil meditation, and the choice of *glimpse* defines the attitude as one of casual
receptivity rather than studious observation. In this mood, Wright
finds the key to his meditation by seeing the river as possessing "its
own secret light." This figure becomes not only a structure for this
piece, but a metaphor that extends to all the descriptive prose.
Wright has become the poet of light, a delicate and sensitive recorder
of subtle shades. He observes a "startling woman," a stranger, in the
park, and he sees her beauty as a secret of light:

Her hair is as black as the inmost secret of light in a perfectly cut diamond,
a perilous black, a secret light that must have been studied for many years
before the anxious and disciplined craftsman could achieve the necessary balance between courage and skill to stroke the strange stone and take the one
chance he would ever have to bring that secret to light. (*BPT*, 38)

The analogy between the diamond cutter and the poet, each having
but one chance to bring a particular secret to light, is important, but
the passage emphasizes, with its repetition connecting light to se-
crecy, the unapproachable but essential truth of the other person manifested metaphorically by the light of the stranger's hair.

The departure of the woman leads Wright to intensify the metaphor associating her exceptional hair with her secret life and to reflect
on the process that necessarily excludes us from ever knowing the secrets of our fellow human beings: "I am afraid her secret might never
come to light in my lifetime. But my lifetime is not the only
one. . . . I hope she brings some other man's secret face to light, as
somebody brought mine" (*BPT*, 38). Rather than feel threatened by
his own inevitable exclusion, Wright patiently accepts that the "inmost secret" of this stranger will be revealed to someone else, entirely
independent of the poet's perception or participation. She will "place
a flawless and fully formed Italian daybreak into the hands" of someone the poet will never know, and he has no regret that the "light
still hidden inside his body is no business of mine." The piece ends
with a tone that characterizes the final volumes: "It is all right with
me to know that my life is only one life. I feel like the light of the
river Adige" (*BPT*, 39).

This acceptance of mortality and the transiency of beauty distinguishes the final volumes from Wright's earlier work. He had always
wanted to be a poet of affirmation, but his fundamental honesty had
often forced him to write poems about despair and frustration. In the

late volumes, he was able to become the poet he had always wanted to be, a poet of light. Both the prose and poetry explore ways we can absorb light. Many of the early poems are permeated with darkness, but now his visual imagery centers on subtle shades of light, whether he contemplates a startling vista in Florence or Verona, a cliffside in Maui, a desert in Arizona, or a hillside in Martins Ferry. This delicate recording usually leads, as in "The Secret of Light," to metaphor. Rainbows are "a miracle of light," light becomes "avenues," "We breathe light," and we sit "On top of the sunlight" in various poems and prose from *This Journey*.

This emphasis on light connotes a patient acceptance of the separation of man and nature. Whereas his mystical impulse had pushed toward complete identification with nature in the earlier books, and the poems often recorded disappointment at the failure of this identification, Wright's new poems record momentary and fragile instances of participation in, and revelation of, the mysterious processes of nature and the secret lives of others. As in "The Secret of Light," this acceptance of the otherness of nature and fellow human beings complements Wright's frequent theme of respecting the privacy of our fellow creatures.

Almost all the prose in *Moments of the Italian Summer* begins in description and moves to meditation. Many meditations in the last two collections are organized around anecdote rather than description. These begin with a memory, but rather than move directly into metaphor, Wright uses the flexibility of prose to allow for the incorporation of a variety of supporting details and to make his judgments explicit. These anecdotal prose pieces often flesh out Wright's regional myth, but the tone is generally more tolerant than that of the Ohio poems in *Two Citizens*. The prose poem often allows Wright to exploit one of his native gifts as a speaker, that of the humorous raconteur.

Wit and playful insolence mark "The Wheeling Gospel Tabernacle." For this cheerful, folksy anecdote, Wright moves beyond personal memory to an incident his parents witnessed two years before he was born. A famous revivalist and his "psalmist and shill at the offeratory," Homer Rhodeheaver, conducted a service in Wheeling, and Wright delights in telling of an interruption during the offering. Police from Pittsburgh raced south to arrest Homer on paternity charges, but the revivalists made a quick exit to places unknown. Wright speculates that they did not ascend toward Heaven, but "skinned the populace" in a nearby town and that "possibly Homer had time between hymns to make some lonely widow happy" (*BPT*, 10).

Cheerful irreverence flavors the anecdote, but Wright also records its value as folklore in a community soon to be victimized by economic problems and comments on the utility of laughter to people subject to economic necessity. "My mother and father got one of their chances to laugh like hell for the sheer joy of laughter before the Great Depression began" at the expense of the embarrassed revivalists. Although Wright is critical of evangelists and delights in their humiliation, his humor is fresh and good-natured. Readers who remember the condemnation of "the insane Jesus Jumpers" in "Ohio Valley Swains" will see how far humor brings him toward tolerance. He even speculates that Homer's erotic love may have the same roots as his professed love for God, and he therefore does not reject his shared humanity with Homer. He actually rejoices in it: "I can pitch a pretty fair tune myself, for all I know" (*BPT*, 10).

Among the most valuable anecdotal prose pieces for students of Wright's poetry is "The Flying Eagles of Troop 62." This begins humorously at the expense of a kind scoutmaster who tolerates secret erotic yearnings and public disrespect for the scouts' oath among his charges. The humor gives way to wonder at the generosity of a man like Ralph Neal, and in his tribute to Neal's decency Wright is able to give specific definition to his phrase "that good man." Throughout his career, this phrase was used as an axiom, but Wright had not given it specific signification until this anecdote. He came very close in "The Old WPA Swimming Pool in Martins Ferry, Ohio," and "Paul," but in both poems the epithet refers to attitudes governing a single act or gesture. In "The Flying Eagles," Neal is portrayed as someone who continuously loves his charges in spite of their misbehavior, and without specific reference to what each would make of his life. The five youths mentioned by Wright took quite different paths. One drives a milk truck, and another works in a steel mill. Two live on the fringes of the law. The last became "something . . . though I don't know just what. Scribbling my name in books" (*BPT*, 15).

Neal's decency is a mystery. Wright mentions the Vedantas and Plato's *Symposium* to explain through philosophy the loyalty Neal extended to his undeserving charges. These do not explain it, because Neal is neither Socrates nor a Hindu mystic, and because mysteries are by definition beyond explanation. Neal's kindness leads Wright to a more comprehensive mystery, the presence of kindness in a society generally committed to self-interest and Philistinism:

I feel a rush of long fondness for that good man Ralph Neal, that good man who knew us dreadful and utterly vulnerable little bastards better than we knew ourselves, who took care of us better than we took care of ourselves, and who loved us, I reckon, because he knew damned well what would become of most of us, and it sure did, and he knew it, and he loved us anyway. The very name of America often makes me sick, and yet Ralph Neal was an American. The country is enough to drive you crazy. (*BPT*, 15–16)

This is Wright's farewell to the wrath of *Two Citizens*. Any generalization, especially one based on feeling rather than thought, is useful only if exceptions to it are few, and exceptions like Ralph Neal can redeem the self-interest of an entire culture. We can lose our minds if we try to reconcile the decency of individuals with the rapacity of multitudes. Perhaps the sanest option is to recognize the fallibility of our generalizations and to rejoice that some of them permit exceptions.

A Recovery of Traditional Forms

The final major collections employ a wide variety of forms. The impulse toward open forms, which dominates every book since *Saint Judas,* reaches its logical limit in the prose. There, Wright adapts form completely to content, to the extent that he abandons altogether the traditional line. Many of the finest poems continue with the free forms sustained by loyalty to the iambic line, in turn adjusted to the demands of conversational tone, that marked *The Branch Will Not Break.* A significant number, however, employ the traditional forms of Wright's first books.

Wright makes more frequent use of traditional meters and stanza arrangements than he had since 1959. "With the Shell of a Hermit Crab," for example, is composed of five iambic tetrameter quatrains, and the rhyme scheme, employing three approximate and seven exact rhymes, is consistent with the form. The poem addresses the theme of mutability, and its form is appropriately one that has traditionally been used to express this theme. Treating a similar subject in a slightly less traditional form, "In Defense of Late Summer" juxtaposes iambic and trochaic trimeter and tetrameter lines to communicate the poet's intense loyalty to the images of summer, expressed as shades of light, which become emblems of life opposed to the gray autumn associated with death.

This Journey as well contains poems made of traditional meters and forms. "Between Wars" employs rhyme in two stanzas of eight lines and one of four. Alternating rhyme organizes these quatrains of iambic tetrameter with trochaic and dactylic variations. The contrast between the ordered arrangement of lines and the chaos of the scene described is effective. The images describe the destruction of an ecosystem, as sparrows eat insects and hawks attack sparrows. As each species destroys another to survive, Wright implies a time when there will be no food to sustain any species. He emphasizes this thought by ending each longer stanza with an overstatement like "There are no insects any more." This elegiac tone, so suited to the traditional rhyme and meter of the poem, is gradually replaced by irony, when the wars in nature are viewed as "earth leaving itself alone." This subtle combination of elegiac tone and entropic theme gains force from Wright's unobtrusive manipulation of poetic conventions.

Wright had avoided the sonnet, one of the most flexible but demanding conventions in English poetry, since he created an original adaptation for "Saint Judas." He returns to the sonnet to record the disappointment he felt when he visited Italy for the last time. "Reading a 1979 Inscription on Belli's Monument" laments the desecration of Belli's "fashionable stone" by one of the "latest Romans" who "bravely climbed his pedestal" to scrawl an obscenity. In the sestet, he pledges a separate communion with Belli by appealing to the forgiving power of nature. His hope that the essence of Belli be spared the ignominy of the present is effectively expressed by adapting a literary convention used to deal with social and cultural issues by such masters as Milton, Shelley, Meredith, Robinson, and Lowell.

This return to traditional forms is not really a radical move on Wright's part. He was always vigorously concerned with form, even while his own compositions adjusted the poetic line to conform with the subject he was treating. During the 1970s, his interest in the classic Latin poets began to exert a stronger influence on his own poetics. He addresses a poem to Horace in that least Horatian of his books, *Two Citizens,* and he mentions Catullus often in the prose pieces and in "One Last Look at the Adige: Verona in the Rain." The epigraph for "With the Shell of a Hermit Crab" comes from one of Catullus's Lesbia poems. The Latin curse in the final section of "Ars

Poetica" has overtones of Virgil. Two companion poems in *To a Blossoming Pear Tree* use a single epigraph from Virgil.

Wright translates *Optima dies prima fugit,* from the *Georgics,* as "The
best days are the first / To flee" in both "The Best Days" and "The
First Days." He had paraphrased the same sentiment in "Eclogue at
Nash's Grove." The elegiac tone of the epigraph notwithstanding,
each poem is a celebration of life. "The Best Days" rejoices in the
dignity and efficiency of two Italian laborers who move a formidable
stone, and Wright draws this wisdom from their effort: "Work hard,
and give / The body its due of rest even at noon" (*BPT,* 51). By seeing Ohio reflected in the beauty of Verona, and by celebrating the
dignity with which the laborers go about their task, Wright counters
the deterministic implications of the epigraph. If the best days pass
first, Wright reasons, the proper attitude is appreciation and enjoy-
ment of those days. It is no accident that one of the expert workers
is an older man.

"The First Days" offers a more ambivalent response to the epigraph. It is a witty anecdote about Wright's intervention to save a
bee from drowning in the juice of a pear it had invaded. Slicing the
fallen pear enough that the bee could escape probably saved its life.
Wright's poem questions his decision to interfere on behalf of the
bee. He prefaces his translation of the epigraph with, "Maybe I
should have left him alone there, / Drowning in his own delight"
(*BPT,* 52). The bee would, like the "Small Frogs Killed on the Highway," have had a glorious death rather than a long life in the polluted
air of "the gasworks at the edge of Mantua." Its best days were its
successful plunge into the fatally delicious nectar, and Wright's analogy suggests that our own best days may be followed by dullness and
despair.

It is likely that Wright's renewed enthusiasm for Virgil, Horace,
and Catullus revived his appreciation for the traditional forms he had
employed in his youth. His return to Horatian decorum was at the
least an artistic manifestation of the tolerance, generosity, and serenity of the final volumes of his poems.

Blossoms from a Pear Tree

Although *To a Blossoming Pear Tree* does not exhibit quite as obvious a principle of internal unity as *The Branch Will Not Break* or *Shall
We Gather at the River,* it, along with those two volumes, forms the

cornerstone of Wright's achievement. The poems do not create, through their dialogic relation one with another, the same unity Wright achieved in the other pivotal collections, but they often form smaller resonating units of meaning, like "The First Days" and "The Best Days" or "To a Blossoming Pear Tree" and "Hook." Wright himself thought this was his finest accomplishment. He felt that it "is the best written and, whatever it says, whatever the value of the book, it is the book that I wanted to write."[7]

We have seen that the book initiates a refinement in attitude and a softened, more subtle style. In a career marked by revolutions in subject matter and form, this quieter revolution seems to have brought its creator the greatest satisfaction. Although literary historians will probably prefer *The Branch Will Not Break* because of its importance in the development of postmodern poetry, *To a Blossoming Pear Tree* rivals even this book in intrinsic excellence.

One reason for the more delicate tones and the more optimistic mood is that Wright's wrath, all but spent in *Two Citizens,* gives way to a reasoned understanding of his relation with his home country. Whereas the former collection distinguished sharply between the quality of life in Europe and America, the author now seeks to integrate those experiences. America is no longer a source of embarrassment for the poet. Wright can at last acknowledge his kinship with the "Sixteen thousand and five hundred more or less people / In Martins Ferry, my home, my native country" in a poem with the revealing but ironic title, "Beautiful Ohio" (*BPT,* 62). Like the cultures they inhabit, these "more or less people" are neither perfect nor fatally flawed. They are simply human. Wright now sees Europe as a mirror for America, and in that glass he sees much to be praised, and condemned, in each culture.

One connection between America and Europe is the subject of "One Last Look at the Adige: Verona in the Rain." This poem is similar in style and structure to several prayers in *Shall We Gather at the River.* The Adige stirs the poet's imagination to reflect on the pristine beauty of the Ohio, "Long before I was born" and before human rapacity scarred the valley. He has not himself experienced this unspoiled beauty in his native land, but because he sees it preserved near Verona, he infers from local legends about islands in the Ohio that such beauty once prompted the inhabitants to create metaphors attributing humanity to the landscape. That the American river was fouled while the Adige was not leads Wright to a condemnation reminiscent of the previous two collections:

> Steubenville is a black crust, America is
> A shallow hell where evil
> Is an easy joke, forgotten
> In a week.
>
> (*BPT*, 5–6)

This sounds like the anger that punctuated Wright's work since "Two Poems About President Harding," but the emphasis immediately shifts from cultural disillusionment to a consideration of a universal dilemma, our individual participation in the passage of time. Wright accepts his fate as a "half-witted angel drawling Ohioan / In the warm Italian rain" and sees his own situation reflected in that of another poet who became a voluntary exile from his native place, Catullus, who "left home and went straight / To hell in Rome" (*BPT*, 6). This allusion is ironic as well as humorous. Had Catullus stayed in Verona, he would never have become involved with Clodia, and spared the conflicting emotions of her spell, he would not have immortalized his feelings in the Lesbia poems.

Exile becomes a central metaphor in this poem. It reflects the problem of accepting our mortality. A cluster of metaphors, the dominant one recalling "The Jewel," allows the poet to describe his existential exile:

> In the middle of my own life
> I woke up and found myself
> Dying, fair enough, still
> Alive in the friendly city
> Of my body, my secret Verona,
> Milky and green,
> My moving jewel, the last
> Pure vein left to me.
>
> (*BPT*, 6)

Although these lines have been seen as a flaw in the beautiful promise and conclusion of the poem because they "convey a loneliness so extreme that it dotes on itself,"[8] the key phrase "fair enough" contributes a tone of resignation to an inevitable process and a determination

to make the most of what is left of our lives. It is true that these
figures convey loneliness, but it is a loneliness we all share when we
realize that our fate is to live and die separately. Wright is not being
self-indulgent here. He responds to a universal dilemma through his
ability to extend his own feelings through metaphor.

That extension is eloquently realized in the final set of metaphors.
As in "The Minneapolis Poem," Wright takes a position that affords
him a perspective on the problem of mortality. He stands on a stone
bridge, "alone, / A dark city on one shore, / And, on the other, / A
dark forest" (BPT, 6–7). Literal imagery becomes metaphor for an existential predicament. The dark forest suggests death and oblivion,
and the dark city implies the imperfect human community Wright
has mourned in many poems. The poet, like all sensible human beings, is caught between the two, but his mood is acceptance, not
defiance.

Similar in structure and subject, but opposite in mood, "Redwings" contemplates our technological ability to control the environment. Whereas "The Adige" began with imagery and moved toward
interpretation of the pattern suggested by the images, "Redwings"
begins with an alarming thesis that the poet's nephew discovered
while writing a scientific report:

> It turns out
> You can kill them.
> It turns out
> You can make the earth absolutely clean.
>   (BPT, 3)

Wright counters this thesis with memories of the delicate beauty of
the redwings we now eliminate as pests, and he sets into motion his
contrast between technological and natural. "Ohio was already going
to hell" because an open sewer poured into the river, and today "dead
gorges / Of highway construction" wreck the landscape. "Going to
hell" has social as well as ecological implications. A childhood sweet-
heart married a strip miner, and her five children are "Floating near
the river" in a spiritual vacuum.

The poem of course sides with the victims, and it draws paranoid
inferences: "Somebody is on the wing, somebody / Is wondering right
at this moment / How to get rid of us, while we sleep" (BPT, 4).
This paranoia is qualified by a memory and a development of the central equation. The poet remembers a hobo who once shared his mea-

ger food and cash with the child, and this kindness, specific and not theoretical, gains emphasis by its being the final gesture in the poem. More convincingly, Wright identifies human beings with the redwings, who continue to fly "across highways and drive / Motorists crazy" in spite of human potential to eliminate them. This suggests that the ability to destroy them is theoretical, but birds do survive to defy that theory. If these pests exhibit such capacity for survival, it must also hold for human beings threatened by real or imagined conspiracies.

The equation between our ability to control the environment and a fundamental contamination of the spirit is explored confessionally in "On a Phrase from Southern Ohio." Like several of the prose pieces, this is anecdotal in structure, but certain phrases lend credibility to Yenser's observation that it is a "sarcastic response" to Dylan Thomas's celebration of the innocent joys of childhood, "Fern Hill."[9] Certainly Wright intends his readers to hear echoes of Thomas in the lines "It is summer chilblain, it is blowtorch, it is not / Maiden and morning on the way up that cliff. / Not where I come from" (*BPT*, 324). He emphatically denies the relevance of Thomas's belief that Eden seems to be recovered in a morning that is "Adam and maiden," itself an echo of the enthusiasm of Hopkins and Traherne. The description of the ascent of the cliff, "We / Climbed / Straight up / And white," while recalling Williams in the visual sense of line, echoes the ascent of the barn ladder in Thomas's final stanza.

The allusion to Thomas sets the mood for Wright's development of two versions of the fall from innocence. The mountain itself has almost been replaced in the poet's memory by blowtorches, the sound of jackhammers, and the slab the workmen poured on the hillside, its purpose unknown and its fate decay. Even then, the slab did not entirely overcome the persistence of nature to renew itself. When the poet and his companions, not the innocent playing children of Thomas's poem but a gang that stole a boat and trespassed, climb the slab, they find bloodroot and "a vicious secret / Of trilliums, . . . the only / Beauty we found, outraged in that naked hell" (*BPT*, 35). The ambiguity of the participle *outraged*, which can describe literally the boy's attitude toward the slab and by personification the attitude of the flowers that continue to grow in these inhospitable circumstances, forms a graceful transition to the principal narrative.

Dedicated to Etheridge Knight, this is a confession and a lament of a collective loss of innocence, racism in America. The seven boys found two black youths near the slab, and "Well, we beat the hell out of one / And chased out the other" (*BPT*, 35). This brutality is quite the opposite of the play Thomas describes in "Fern Hill," but Wright's point is not to refute Thomas. He seeks to come to terms with the heritage of a guilt at least as insidious as the greed that causes men to gouge out hillsides. He personally carries both individual and collective guilt for a society that has an unenviable history of racism: "And still in my dreams I sway like one fainting strand / Of spiderweb, glittering and vanishing and frail / Above the river" (*BPT*, 35). This echo of Whitman's "Noiseless Patient Spider" works both ironically and literally. The boys certainly failed to make the human connections Whitman desires, but Wright, in this appeal to a distinguished black poet, tries to make a connection that bridges personal culpability as well as many generations of conflict.

Not generations but centuries of conflict are the background of one of Wright's finest poems, "Written on a Big Cheap Postcard from Verona." The witty title and the structure recall distinctive work in *The Branch Will Not Break*. This communication from Verona to America includes European politics that are at least as sordid as American, but it finally transcends the political to affirm both life in the face of certain defeat of our aspirations and the power of art to capture our aspirations toward transcendence.

The occasion for this reflection is the postcard of the title, the type most of us have mailed from tourist traps. A Veronese card would logically celebrate the two most famous fictional citizens of the city, but Wright has no illusions about the artistic value of his card. He, or anyone, can "buy romantical junk" like this cheaply in a tourist trap "And send vulgarity home." We should note in passing a reversal of Wright's characteristic attitude. Now the junk is produced and bought in Europe, and vulgarity moves in a direction opposite from that implied in many earlier poems. He knows the card is a garish, commercial exploitation of literature, but his imagination ranges freely over the essence Shakespeare captured that in turn made Romeo and Juliet immortal enough to adorn cheap postcards.

This free range of imagination gives structure to the poem. The lovers have become immortal embodiments of mysterious beauty in a world accustomed to violence and vulgarity. How to explain that immortality engages the poet in a debate between reason and intuition. Romeo and Juliet are not legendary because of their specific deeds or the facts we know about them. They are intuitive symbols for a mystery. The average person will remember only

> a radiance in the dusk,
> A light wing fluttering in a vine,
> Hands shocked by touching,
> Strange and forbidden,
> A bomb, and no chance
> To live long.
>
> (*BPT,* 42)

These metaphors suggest that we remember impressions, not facts, about the lovers. Their brilliance in dreary surroundings is fated to sudden brief glory, and there is something dangerous to the status quo, as well as beautiful, in what they mean.

The facts about Shakespeare's story simply do not add up to this kind of radiance. When reason turns its harsh light on the lovers, it discloses sordid details about family conflicts, street warfare, "One pointless murder after another," a marriage practical parents would probably have annulled, "And the absolutely final death, ridiculous, / Brutal, a cheap loss, a death cruel / And stupid as yours or mine" (*BPT,* 41). These details, which reason can summarize, cannot tell us much about the "clear genius" Shakespeare applied to "his fierce cold play" or the radiance everyone associates with his tragic lovers.

Wright organizes the rest of the poem around the phrase "I know," by which he communicates the limits of reason to comprehend what Shakespeare's lovers mean to us. We can "know" the sources of this and other plays, and that knowledge may lead us to contemplate Shakespeare's improvements on Arthur Brooke's "mediocre narrative poem" or Thomas Greene's prose romance, but this will not get us to the meaning of his lovers. We may learn about Veronese history, where we find occasional rebellion and, in our time, brutal, destructive bombings the city was somehow able to survive. This too adds to our knowledge of the context of Romeo and Juliet, but it does not account for their "radiance."

The poet modestly downplays his own invention as a "gross and messy imitation" of Shakespeare's dream, but in that confession, he endorses a fundamental Shakespearian truth that effectively explains the permanence of the tragic lovers. They are

>   a poet's dream of something hopeless
>   That didn't have a chance in this world.
>   What chance do we have?
>   We are nothing but a poet's dream
>   Of lovers who chose to live.
>   Not a chance.
>
>   (*BPT*, 43)

Wright deliberately echoes the phrasing of two of Shakespeare's dukes who organize love-matches. Theseus, in *A Midsummer Night's Dream*, tells his bride that "as imagination bodies forth / The forms of things unknown, the poet's pen / Turns them to shapes and gives to airy nothing / A local habitation and a name" (5.1.14–17). Shakespeare in *Romeo and Juliet* and Wright in this poem do indeed give a "local habitation" to our collective dream that love must be greater than the outward circumstances that affect it.

Directly echoed in Wright's lines are Prospero's comments to the young lovers in *The Tempest* about the relation of reality and illusion. He tells them "We are such stuff / As dreams are made on, and our little life / Is rounded with a sleep" (4.1.156–58). By insisting, as Prospero does, on the identification of human beings with creations of art, Wright suggests that the very quality of our lives, the ability to be fully human, depends on our responding to the dreams of our greatness, even in the face of certain defeat in the practical eyes of the world.

This is clear in the coda of Wright's poem. Repeating his phrase about the limits of rationality, "I know," he balances realism against the imaginative ideal of the lovers. Realism tells us an entropic tale at least as grim as Prospero's: "The world is a mess, / A sinking menace of loveliness and danger" (*BPT*, 43). This is a perception we cannot afford to ignore. But we need art because it is the poet's dream that captures our collective faith in a truth that transcends brute facts and that persists in the face of our awareness of all the ugly, stupid, chintzy facts with which we must try to live.

Wright returns in memory to the scene of his most despairing poetry, Minneapolis, for the central poems of the collection. "Hook" and the title poem resonate against one another, and although each can be appreciated as a self-contained work of art, they are best read as variations on the questions of love, fraternity, and our potential relation with nature. Together or separately, these add conclusive evidence to the main concern of this chapter, the degree to which the poet's wiser and more forgiving attitude toward himself as an American contributed to his writing some of his best poetry.

"Hook" may be read as a counter-statement to the pessimism of "The Minneapolis Poem" and "I Am a Sioux Brave, He Said in Minneapolis" because it emphasizes generosity and brotherhood in a city Wright had associated with alienation. He recalls a winter of his own discontent, in which the "dead snow," the slashing wind, and the "terrible starlight" create a pathetic fallacy for the despair the young poet, "in trouble / With a woman," was feeling. In the first stanza, the word *nothing* is repeated three times to emphasize the nihilistic attitude he felt because of his personal problems.

The despair of his personal situation yields to a chance encounter with a young Indian, whose "scars / Were just my age." The Sioux has a prosthetic hand, and he tells the poet that the injury was the result of trouble with a woman. They share a problem, and the Indian's hook tells Wright that such difficulties will be overcome in time, even if they may leave permanent scars. The Indian's attitude, moreover, suggests the possibility of a forgiving acceptance of the difficulties life imposes upon us.

This possibility is communicated to the reader by the poet's acceptance of sixty-five cents from the Indian. Wright reverses the attitude of "The Offense," in which he accused a friend of imposing an unnecessary loan on him, because he recognizes that the Indian is giving him something far more important than money: "I took it. / It wasn't the money I needed. / But I took it" (*BPT,* 59). The poet "needed" the example of the Sioux's acceptance of his own plight as well as the concern the young Indian, himself the victim of several "scars," willingly offered a white stranger who has never known the special frustration the Sioux, a member of a cultural minority, has had to overcome in addition to the problems they share. The sixty-five cents, passed "Gently" from the hook to the poet's "freezing hand," is among the richest symbols in recent poetry. It suggests the generosity of spirit, the capacity to forgive, and the willingness to share meager resources with strangers that distinguishes human life from that of a beast. It cannot be proved that such ethical action is necessary, but it is axiomatic that we need instances like "Hook" to remind us of our human potential. Shakespeare, whom Wright had invoked in "Big Cheap Postcard," drew the same conclusion in *King Lear:* "Allow not nature more than nature needs, / Man's life is cheap as beast's" (2.4.265–66). Human life may be impoverished and frustrated in "Hook," but it is anything but cheap.

The poet receives unexpected human friendship in "Hook," but in "To a Blossoming Pear Tree" a degenerate homosexual approached the poet with a desperate plea for love. This poem, somewhat more complex in structure than "Hook," is a prayer to a tree, something serenely above any human need for love. Wright occupies an intermediary position on the moral scale, between the perfect self-sufficiency of the tree and the despair of the old man. His memory of an appeal for love that offended him leads to an evaluation of the claims of a perfect but distant nature and of a flawed human relationship.

His appeal to the self-sufficient beauty of the tree reminds us of Jeffers's inhumanist doctrine. While Wright admires and yearns for that perfect state beyond the turbulence of human emotions, he reluctantly accepts his shared humanity with the loveless homosexual. He envies the serenity of the tree, yet he feels that the tree needs to learn from human beings: "For if you could only listen, / I would tell you something, / Something human" (*BPT*, 60). The problem with the serenity of the tree is that it is self-sufficient and therefore self-contemplative:

> Beautiful natural blossoms
> How could you possibly
> Worry or bother or care
> About the ashamed, hopeless
> Old man?
>   (*BPT*, 60–61)

This indifference is the result of perfection or serenity, and Wright, forced to make his choice, affirms his humanity with even this sad old man whose plea terrified him years before.

He does not rejoice in his intermediary position, but he accepts it as the fate of caring human beings:

> Young tree, unburdened
> By anything but your beautiful natural blossoms
> And dew, the dark
> Blood in my body drags me
> Down with my brother.
>   (*BPT*, 61)

The choice is between perfection and process, and Wright makes the only choice his art will allow. We may regret our shared imperfection. We may be repelled by the forms the need for love takes in others. To acknowledge our bond with this man is also to accept our loneliness and mortality. Wright's mature compassion requires nothing less of us if we expect to call ourselves human beings.

Stages on *This Journey*

To a Blossoming Pear Tree was the last volume of poems Wright published in his lifetime. It was the most satisfying to the poet, and further generations will consider it central to his achievement. A final collection, however, was all but complete before he entered the hospital early in 1980. In fact, a few of these poems had appeared in the James Wright issue of *Ironwood* in 1977. Shortly before his death he sent copies of the manuscript to several of his friends for their comments. Almost five months after Wright's death, Donald Hall and his wife Jane Kenyon joined Anne Wright at the Vermont home of Galway Kinnell to discuss the publication of *This Journey*. They considered the comments of the friends to whom Wright had sent the typescript, deleted a few poems, added one from Wright's last work, and brought out the final volume.

A sentimental aura, therefore, surrounds *This Journey,* as the deathbed collection of a distinguished poet. This is not really warranted, because Wright had finished almost all the poems before his condition disabled him. He devoted most of his attention during the months before the late stage of his illness to teaching and to writing material for *The Summers of James and Annie Wright,* a collection of eleven prose pieces by James and four by Annie. This book also came into print after Wright's death. Yet it is doubtful that any number of facts will ever remove the solemnity of a deathbed collection from *This Journey.* The poems maintain the tone of patient acceptance and wisdom that marked *Pear Tree,* and the inescapable impression is that of a poet grown wise and confident in his craft summarizing and synthesizing his artistic and cultural concerns of more than a quarter of a century.

This impression is further supported by the mood of the poems about the home country. The Ohio poems of the previous volume exhibited a tolerance for the fallibility of all human institutions, but those in the final book are overtly elegiac. They remark on the passing of people and landmarks of Wright's youth and by implication the passing of the way of life Wright both loved and despised.

"Chilblain" laments once more the death of Wright's uncle Willy Lyons, one of the central characters of the poet's regional myth. This poem is less somber than the famous elegy in *Shall We Gather at the River*. It shares the flavor of the reminiscence "On the Occasion of a Poem: Bill Knott,"[10] which treats Lyons as a local character. Here Willy is a purveyor of bogus folklore about a salve he found in "them cathouses" in France during "the big war." It did not cure chilblain but "stung so bad it took / Your mind off your troubles" (*TJ*, 25). Wright tenderly recalls the teasing of the children by this oddball with the "long lecherous face" and the silent snicker that implied a "proud man's wisdom," but his dreams are haunted by his uncle's death. "Willy the liar is buried in Colrain," and neither his lechery nor his teasing now matters except in memory. The slag heaps, synecdoches for a dreary future in Ohio since "Stages on a Journey Westward," continue to steam, and the violets like Willy's life "last only a little" in the region of his birth and his uncle's grave. Wright excuses Willy's faults, but he recognizes the persistence of those pains with which we all live and seek means to alleviate, even if we know those means are fraudulent.

The cryptic "In Memory of Mayor Richard Daley" is a more generalized elegy. The title leads readers to expect a political poem concerning the career of the Chicago boss whom Wright once listed among the powerful individuals who have "fooled around with the language for quite some time," but with whom it "gets even . . . frequently."[11] Neither the boss nor his career is mentioned in the poem, but the title suggests by analogy an elegiac concern with the passing of power and the levelling of all human striving in death.

The structure owes something to Frost's "Directive," in which the poet guides the reader on a journey to a scene of ruin. Wright echoes Frost's diction, "And there in the river's graveyard / Nobody moves any more but you and me" (*TJ*, 52), as he leads his reader to scenes of decay at the outskirts of Martins Ferry, where tough weeds persist "like the mystery / Of cancer," and a waste space where a "rum-bum" carelessly set fire to a lumber yard. Once, when the young Wright and some friends came to the spot "to sing drunk," they stumbled on the focal point of the desolate landscape. A slab of gritstone at the center of the scene has fallen, and the name has been eroded by years of weather, but this anonymity is countered by local folklore Wright chooses not to share with his readers. If his narrative, like the title, is cryptic, the meaning of the stone is not. Metaphorically, the stone becomes a face and therefore may link with Daley, whose arrogant features were printed in many newspapers and magazines, and both the face and stone are called "a precious thing." Like Lyons, it fills the poet's dream as a *memento mori:*

> I can't get away from it.
> This face fills me with grief as I sing to myself
> In my sleep: Remember, remember,
> This is what you're up against.
>
> *(TJ,* 53).

It reminds the poet not only of the death we all must face, but of the fleeting nature of fame and achievement.

The local legend of the configuration of the LaBelle Lumber Company is mentioned again in "A Flower Passage *(in memory of Joe Shank, the diver)."* This comprehensive elegy for Wright's lost youth contributes to the impression that *This Journey* is a deliberate culmination of the poet's work. He admits that he would not be recognized by Shank, a local hero who earned his reputation by diving in the river and recovering, among other things, the bodies of drowned swimmers. By the standards of local reputation, he realizes that his youth as "one of the briefly green" would be indistinguishable to Shank from the "other / Children of the blast furnace and mine [who] / Fought and sang in the channel-current / Daring the Ohio" *(TJ,* 56).

The poem mourns the passing of Shank, as both hero and "Shepherd of the dead," who has now been "turned over / To the appropriate authorities," and with a proper elegiac convention the poet sees in Shank's death the fate of all human beings: "Christ / Have mercy on me." Calling the subject of the elegy a shepherd as Milton does in "Lycidas," Wright ironically invokes an accompanying pastoral convention, the procession of mourners. Because he is "not home in my place / Where I was born and my friends drowned" both literally and metaphorically, he cannot bring his offering of carnations to the funeral home. As a substitute, the poet offers in imaginative tribute to Shank and "my drowned friends" the true, if pedestrian, vegetation peculiar to Ohio like "blind and tough / Fireweeds," "true sumac," and "foul trillium." These are not traditional flowers of mourning, but Wright will later "bring / The still totally unbelievable spring beauty / That for some hidden reason nobody raped / To death in Ohio" (*TJ*, 57).

The flowers Wright offers and the more traditional ones he will later bring have this in common: they are survivors of harsh conditions and human folly. The poet too has survived not only spiritual drowning in the Ohio basin, but also his hatred of that environment. This is a perfect farewell to Wright's Ohio poems in that he is able to reconcile himself to the imperfectability of his home country and to pay his ultimate tribute by acknowledging that his escape can never be complete.

Pastoral conventions are employed with loving irony in "A Flower Passage." In other poems in the collection the poet finds new uses for this vital poetic tradition. "Notes of a Pastorialist" humorously compares a modern Italian shepherd with the shepherds of literary convention. This shepherd leans on an incongruous green umbrella rather than a tree, and his sheep do "not flock together / As they do in Spenser and Theocritus" (*TJ*, 14). Wright cheerfully admits that the literary convention is really a metaphor for our desire to return to innocence, whereas the real shepherd pipes notes "Of a jaded pastoralist." The humor is balanced by a recognition that commercialism has replaced the pastoral vision. He hopes the shepherd pleased himself with his song, because "I didn't feel / Like paying him to sing" (*TJ*, 14). The insidious materialism of the modern world seems to have invaded the last bastion of innocence, the pastures of shepherds.

Since the experiment in "Saint Judas," Wright had used the dramatic monologue only to unusual circumstances like "Confession to J. Edgar Hoover" or "A Mad Song for William S. Carpenter." His poetic gifts were predominantly lyrical, not dramatic. In "Jerome in Solitude" he returns to the dramatic mode and assumes the voice of a Christian saint to contrast religion based on mortification with a pantheistic appreciation of the divinity of all creation. The historical Saint Jerome underwent a spiritual change after a severe illness and resolved to renounce whatever kept him from God. He zealously advocated renunciation, celibacy, and the monastic life. Wright's learned doctor contemplates, not the challenge of translating the Scriptures, but a lowly lizard. He is "amazed" that this vision comes naturally, not as the result of self-moritification: "I did not have to beat / My breast with a stone" (*TJ*, 72). He is more surprised that this obviously religious experience does not contain images of agony,

"Christ retching in pain," or intimations of the tenuous position human beings occupy between the created and the divine, "Flesh torn between air and air."

Jerome's vision arrests him because of its natural serenity, in which it is impossible to be certain whether one is praying, meditating, or contemplating. In this frozen moment, he studies the lizard—and the lizard studies him—as coexistent proofs of the divinity of creation. The images make it clear that Wright prefers the natural religion Jerome momentarily experiences over more institutional forms, and the title, by suggesting that such a vision can come to the Church Father only "in solitude," implies that Wright intends the poem to comment on an essentially private communion with Creation as the central substance of religious experience.

Always an essentially pantheistic poet influenced by Whitman and Wordsworth, Wright became more interested in divinity manifested in natural experiences during his final years. This concern unifies the prose meditations, the poems about Ohio, those about Hawaii, those concerning the sea, and "Saint Jerome." In fact, the organizing theme of the final collection could be called the tough presence of divinity in even the smallest things. A discussion on four particularly satisfying variations on this theme enables us to comment briefly on the legacy of Wright's poetry as well as its intrinsic merit.

Humor and irony balance pathos in two studies of birds, central symbols throughout Wright's work for the reassuring presence of the divinity of nature. "A Dark Moor Bird" humorously considers the incongruity of the creature's physical beauty and grace against the harsh, funny noise it makes, "Like a plump chicken nagging a racoon / Who is trying to get out of the henhouse / With a little dignity" (*TJ*, 13). Deft irony ultimately celebrates the determination and wisdom of "A Finch Sitting Out a Windstorm," certainly a distant cousin of the marvelous blue jay that supported the poet's faith in "Two Hangovers." Wright appears to complain because the stupid bird does not have enough sense to retreat from the cold wind as a human being chastened by experience would. The poet has learned the "wisdom of hopelessness" from "Too many Maytime snowfalls," and he advises a prudent retreat:

> But the damned fool
> Squats there as if he owned
> The earth, bought and paid for.

> Oh, I could advise him plenty
> About his wings. Give up, drift,
> Get out.
>
> (*TJ*, 62)

Wright really means that the finch's supreme virtue, in addition to its tenacity, is that "He never listens / To me." The poet's advice is worldly wisdom, prudence, retreat. The bird has a superior, instinctive determination to grasp sensuously and directly the whole range of experience, and to accept the price of having its face "battered" like that of a famous and persistent prize fighter.

The insect in "To the Cicada" becomes a constant reminder of the divinity in nature. It is a sufficient symbol to compensate for reason's awareness of the inevitability of human decay and the tendency of human institutions to falsify our impulses toward the divine. Wright organizes this tribute around three clusters of images. One set emphasizes mass and weight, and therefore suggests decay and death. Another focuses on sound, particularly the noises made by the "Holy Rollers" who "rage all afternoon" with their "voices splintering / Like beetles' wings in a hobo jungle fire" to force a revelation of "their brutal / Jesus risen but dumb" (*TJ*, 35). This image shares the bitterness toward evangelical religion of "Ohio Valley Swains" rather than the good-humored acceptance of "The Wheeling Gospel Tabernacle," but the bitterness is an essential part of the set of contrasts Wright invokes to celebrate the constant presence of divinity in nature.

The description of the human body evokes weight and certain movement toward death. The poet's eyelids "weigh ten pounds," his fingers are stiff, and his shoulders "grow heavier and heavier." An airless barn has been cleansed of vegetable and animal waste "jagged and cruel / as old gravestones," and the central simile in this cluster of images associates the human body with meat cured for human consumption: "And the hooks creak as the meat sags, just so / My bones sag and hold up / The flesh of my body" (*TJ*, 35). In this despairing acceptance of the fatal union of our bodies with all creation, it is perhaps some consolation that the hooks and bones, although they sag, do hold.

The imagery describing the cicada incorporates elements from both clusters. Whereas the hymn of the Holy Rollers is harsh, the song of the cicada is constant and soothing; whereas the body and human artifacts are heavy, the cicada is "lightness." The Holy Rollers can try to coerce their Jesus to appear at their jarring service, but the poet can participate in his own miracle by breathing life upon a god of nature:

> You, lightness,
> How were you born in this place, this heavy stone
> Plummeting into the stars?
> And still you are here. . . .
> You, lightness, kindlier than my human body,
> Yet somehow friendly to the music in my body,
> I let you sleep, one of the gods who will rise
> Without being screamed at.
>
> (*TJ*, 36)

Here is the essence of Wright's mature mysticism. The cicada is a god-figure, and it approves and inspires the music within our mortal body, be it the rhythm of the blood or poetry. As part of creation, we can perform a miracle for the god, too. We can breathe our life-giving warmth on a manifestation of God's continuing presence with us.

Another insect, a spider, becomes the occasion of a spiritual experience in "The Journey." From this mystical moment, Wright derives an inference that transforms religious experience to a practical ethical attitude that enables us to face life patiently and creatively. Wright organizes this intensely personal poem, like "To the Cicada," around three sets of images. The picturesque beauty of a medieval city suggests the poet's contemplation of the past, but he is surrounded by a peasant population of children who are the hope of the future. The poet, like most of us, occupies a position between past and future.

Both groups of images share a common denominator, the dust. It covers "everything," the city and the children, as well as the poet who rinses dust from his face. Dust has obvious archetypal signification as sterility and religious association with death. Past, present, and future are covered with this reminder of death, as is the spider's web. Wright's metaphor makes religious and anthropological associations inevitable. The web sways under "mounds and cemeteries of it," but the spider herself, when she comes into view, is "Slender," "fastidious," and "Free of the dust," "While ruins crumbled on every side of her."

The spider's cleanliness isolates her from bondage in time, but she is not a god-figure. Her freedom from dust results from washing, but not in water. Her bathing, implying baptism, is a stepping "inside

the earth." By this Wright suggests a natural state of grace, one confirmed by immersion in nature rather than by institutions. This perception leads Wright to see the spider as "the heart of the light," a
metaphor with religious, even mystical, signification in Eliot's *Four
Quartets* and Dante's *Paradiso*. This religious value enables Wright to
formulate the central inference of all his poetry, an ethical and aesthetic legacy of which any poet can be proud and for which any perceptive reader should be grateful:

> The secret
> Of this journey is to let the wind
> Blow its dust all over your body,
> To let it go on blowing, to step lightly, lightly
> All the way through your ruins, and not to lose
> Any sleep over the dead, who surely
> Will bury their own, don't worry.
>
> (*TJ*, 31)

Chapter Seven
"The Poetry of a Grown Man"

Wright's growth as a poet is a useful paradigm for the development of poetry since the Second World War. This study has attempted to trace the growth of a mind as well as the development of an artistic vision. The poet felt that he had achieved his goal, writing the "poetry of a grown man," in *To a Blossoming Pear Tree,* and it was certainly a goal worth striving for and achieving. As we have seen, this goal demanded constant adjustment in personal vision as well as in poetic technique.

In his beautiful tribute "Lighting a Candle for W. H. Auden," Wright said something that applies to his own as well as to Auden's life: "The poet kept his promise / To the earth before he died" (*BPT,* 22). The promise implies an ability to grow in vision and technique, and an element of Wright's tribute is Auden's turning to Christianity as a way of coming to terms with his existential dilemma. Wright did not make exactly that journey, but his poetry expresses increasingly mature pantheistic and cultural values.

It is clear that Wright will continue to be read as one of the influential poets of his age. His work has been respected and assimilated by most of the important poets of our time. He participated in three major revolutions in poetics, and ultimately went beyond each movement as an individual. His early works are among the most successful of the academic poems that replaced modernism in the decades after World War II. His major volumes are among the finest, as well as most historically important, among the deep image movement, and they integrate elements of the confessional school as well. At the height of his fame, he boldly attempted a major revision of his style, one that led him toward a lean, sometimes abrasive, rhetoric. With *To a Blossoming Pear Tree,* he accomplished a thoroughly original synthesis of the styles and attitudes of all his previous work.

In the final analysis, however, poetic accomplishment cannot be equated with contribution to any number of artistic movements, however historically important each may be. Achievement, and ultimately reputation, can be measured only by the impact of individual poems on a variety of intelligent readers. This means, among other things, the ability to speak through art to those universal sentiments and thoughts we all share regardless of differences in temperament and cultural heritage. Wright's way of addressing these thoughts and emotions seems to me an ideal one. At his best, he captures the tension between thought and feeling by synthesizing them. His poems consistently have the power of a "felt idea" or of a "thought feeling." Several approach the definition of art proposed by Alexander Pope, a poet Wright respected but whose general artistic vision was antithetical to Wright's own: "What oft was thought, but ne'er so well express'd."

This is not to imply that Wright was without any limitations as an artist. He was a passionate individual, and his passion sometimes came into confict with his commitment to classical restraint. Many of the excesses of the "New Poems," *Two Citizens,* and a few poems in *Shall We Gather at the River* can be traced to bitterness characteristic of the Vietnam era, and it is hardly surprising that these were the poems with which Wright was least satisfied. The views are sometimes trendy, and the rhetoric is hyperbolic. The attitudes occasionally are oversimplifications of complex issues, and the emotions are as crude as the rhetoric. This is not to excuse or condemn Wright's choices in a period of passionate simplification. Yet we expect more of a poet than we do of an ordinary citizen. We legitimately expect him to rise above, not to voice, the cliches of his age. Because of Wright's respect for and ability with language, we reasonably expect him to use his art to recognize the shabby and superficial in current intellectual trends as well as in contemporary institutions.

These were inclinations Wright quickly adjusted in his art, and many poems from even this period reward continued reading and reflection. Examining Wright's best work, we discover a powerful, authentic voice. He succeeded remarkably in an astonishing variety of forms, from very open, free verse to effective adaptations of demanding traditional forms. This eclectic achievement promises that readers of many literary tastes will find value in his art.

His themes are consistent, yet varied and original. Few poets of our time have recorded as successfully as Wright the many types of alienation to which human beings are subject. A growing awareness now exists that Wright was also what I called in a previous chapter a poet of light. This pantheistic and humanistic emphasis on moments of rapture occasioned by love or by intense communion with nature is not limited to "A Blessing." It occurs with increasing frequency in the late collections and is powerfully felt in even the most despairing volumes. "Bologna: A Poem About Gold" is, after all, the centerpiece of *Two Citizens*.

What made Wright a poet of lasting stature was a combination of native talent, original vision, appreciation for the possibilities of language, willingness to take risks with his art, total honesty and sincerity, and the unique ability to make his vision, however temporarily, our own.

Notes and References

Chapter One

1. "The Stiff Smile of Mr. Warren," *Kenyon Review* 20 (1958):646. Reprinted in *Collected Prose,* edited by Anne Wright (Ann Arbor: University of Michigan Press, 1983), 239–49. In these notes, this collection is identified as *Prose.*

2. "On the Occasion of a Poem," in *American Poets in 1976,* ed. William Heyen (Indianapolis: Bobbs-Merrill, 1976), 439. Reprinted in *Prose,* 303–9.

3. *This Journey* (New York: Random House 1982), 54. References in the text identify this collection as *TJ.*

4. *Collected Poems* (Middletown, Conn.: Wesleyan University Press, 1971), 208. References in the text identify this collection as *CP.*

5. "The Infidel," in *American Poets in 1976,* 453. Reprinted in *Prose,* 324–29.

6. Annie Wright, "A Horse Grazes in My Long Shadow: A Brief Biography of James Wright," *Envoy,* Spring–Summer 1981, 1.

7. Letters to Theodore Roethke, 13 September 1957; 11 February 1958; to Robert Heilman, 9 December 1957. These are in the Roethke and Heilman collections of the University of Washington libraries.

8. Letter to Heilman, 29 March 1959; from Heilman to Wright, 8 April 1959.

9. "On the Occasion of a Poem: Bill Knott," in *American Poets in 1976,* 441. Reprinted in *Prose,* 310–23.

10. Quoted by Peter Serchuk, "On the Poet, James Wright," *Modern Poetry Studies* 10 (1981):87; Peter Stitt, "The Art of Poetry XIX: James Wright," *Paris Review* 62 (1975):40.

11. Wright, "A Horse Grazes," 4; Anne Wright, "Fragments from a Journey," *Kenyon Review* 7 (Summer 1985):37–39.

12. Dave Smith, "James Wright: The Pure Clear Word, an Interview," in *The Pure Clear Word: Essays on the Poetry of James Wright,* ed. Dave Smith (Urbana: University of Illinois Press, 1982), 12. Interview reprinted in *Prose,* 191–235.

13. Letter to Heilman, 4 January 1958.

14. Joseph R. McElrath, ed., "Something to Be Said for the Light: A Conversation with James Wright," *Southern Humanities Review* 6 (1972):138. Reprinted in *Prose,* 151–71.

15. Letter to Roethke, 5 August 1958.

16. Stitt, "Art of Poetry," 42.

17. Crunk [Robert Bly], "The Work of James Wright," *Sixties* 8 (1966):52–78. Reprinted with an additional note in *Pure Clear Word*, 78–98.

18. Michael Andre, "An Interview With James Wright," *Unmuzzled Ox* 1 (February 1972):3. Reprinted in *Prose*, 133–50.

19. Charles Molesworth, *The Fierce Embrace* (Columbia: University of Missouri Press, 1979), 115.

20. Stitt, "Art of Poetry," 51.

21. "Some Recent Poetry," *Sewanee Review* 66 (1958):659.

Chapter Two

1. See Henry Taylor, "In the Mode of Robinson and Frost: James Wright's Early Poetry," and William Matthews, "The Continuity of James Wright's Poems," *Ohio Review* 18 (Spring-Summer 1977):44–57; reprinted in *Pure Clear Word*, 50, 100–101. See also Madeline DeFrees, "That Vacant Paradise: James Wright's Potter's Field," *Ironwood* 10 (1977):18, and De-Frees, "James Wright's Early Poems: A Study in 'Convulsive Form,' " *Modern Poetry Studies* 2 (1972):241–51.

2. See Smith, "An Interview," 18; McElrath, "Conversation," 139; and Taylor, "In the Mode," 49–50.

3. "An Evening with Ted Roethke," *Michigan Quarterly Review* 6 (1967):234, quoted by James E. B. Breslin, *From Modern to Contemporary: American Poetry, 1945–1965* (Chicago: University of Chicago Press, 1984), 1. For a perceptive discussion of the problems faced by the second generation of postmodern poets, see Breslin's chapter, "The End of the Line."

4. W. H. Auden, foreword to *The Green Wall* (New Haven: Yale University Press, 1957), xiv. Reprinted in *Pure Clear Word*, 46.

5. DeFrees, "Vacant Paradise," 13.

6. See Ralph J. Mills, Jr., "James Wright's Poetry: Introductory Notes," *Chicago Review* 17 (1964):133–35; David C. Dougherty, "The Skeptical Poetic of James Wright," *Contemporary Poetry* 11 (1977):4–10; and Breslin, *From Modern*, 190–93.

7. "The Delicacy of Walt Whitman," in *The Presence of Walt Whitman*, ed. R. W. B. Lewis (New York: Columbia University Press, 1962), 177, 165. Reprinted in *Prose*, 3–22.

8. "Occasion of a Poem," 435–40. In *Ironwood* 10 (1977) and in *This Journey*, Wright published a different account of the trip, "Lament: Fishing with Richard Hugo."

9. Stitt, "Art of Poetry," 45.

10. John Ditsky, "James Wright Collected: Alterations on the Monument," *Modern Poetry Studies* 2 (1972):255; Ralph J. Mills, Jr., *Contemporary American Poetry* (New York: Random House, 1965), 205; Paul A. Lacey, *The*

Inner War: Forms and Themes in Recent American Poetry (Philadelphia: Fortress Press, 1972), 59.

11. The early version appears in *Poetry* 92 (1958–59):277–79; Smith, "An Interview," 21–22.

12. Quoted by Serchuk, "On the Poet," 89.

Chapter Three

1. See Stephen Stepanchev, *American Poetry since 1945* (New York: Harper & Row, 1965), 183; James Seay, "A World Immeasurably Alive and Good: A Look at James Wright's *Collected Poems*," *Georgia Review* 27 (1973), reprinted in *Pure Clear Word*, 113–15; Breslin, *From Modern*, 196; and Paul Zweig, "Making and Unmaking," *Partisan Review* 40 (1973):270.

2. Quoted in DeFrees, "Early Poems," 242; Stitt, "Art of Poetry," 54.

3. Ronald Moran and George Lensing, "The Emotive Imagination: A New Departure in American Poetry," *Southern Review* 3 (1967):53. See also Moran and Lensing, *Four Poets and the Emotive Imagination: Robert Bly, James Wright, Louis Simpson, and William Stafford* (Baton Rouge: Louisiana State University Press, 1976); G. A. M. Jannsens, "The Present State of American Poetry: Robert Bly and James Wright," *English Studies* 51 (1970):127; Breslin, *From Modern*, 194; and Alan Williamson, *Introspection in Contemporary American Poetry* (Cambridge: Harvard University Press, 1984), 66.

4. "A Note on Trakl," *Twenty Poems by Georg Trakl*, trans. Robert Bly and James Wright (Madison, Minn.: Sixties Press, 1961), reprinted in *Prose*, 83; Stitt, "Art of Poetry," 48; Matthews, "Continuity," 106.

5. Williamson, *Introspection*, 70–71, offers a thorough and perceptive reading. Stitt, "The Quest Motif in *The Branch Will Not Break*," in *Pure Clear Word*, 70–71, provides several valuable insights into the ways the poem illuminates the poet's relation with nature in the volume. For an adverse reading of "Hammock," see Stephen Yenser, "Open Secrets," *Parnassus* (1978):125–42, reprinted in *Pure Clear Word*, 141. Bonnie Costello, "James Wright: Returning to the Heartland," *New Boston Review* 5 (1980):12–14, expanded in *Pure Clear Word*, 226, comments on the final line as "an abrupt non sequitur."

6. Herman Hesse, *Wandering*, trans. James and Franz Wright (New York: Farrar, Straus & Giroux, 1972), 6–7.

7. Stitt, "Quest Motif," 66.

8. Robert Hass, "James Wright," *Ironwood* 10 (1977): 74–96, reprinted in *Pure Clear Word*, 210–11. Hass says very insightful things about the speaker.

9. Crunk, "Work of James Wright," 73.

10. Stitt, "Quest Motif," 66–76.

Chapter Four

   1. Zweig, "Making," 20–21; Stitt, "Art of Poetry," 52.
   2. Leonard Nathan, "The Traditional James Wright," *Ironwood* 10 (1977); reprinted in *Pure Clear Word,* 162–63; Costello, "Heartland," 228; Stitt, "Art of Poetry," 43–44.
   3. "On the Occasion of a Poem: Bill Knott," 446–49.
   4. Smith, "An Interview," 36–37.

Chapter Five

   1. Stitt, "Art of Poetry," 56; Smith, "An Interview," 30.
   2. *Two Citizens* (New York: Farrar, Straus & Giroux, 1971), 19. References in the text identify this collection as *TC*.
   3. Similar conclusions are reached in Yenser, "Open Secrets," 140–41.
   4. Williamson, *Introspection,* 83; Dave Smith, "That Halting, Stammering Movement," *Ironwood* 10 (1977):111–30, reprinted in *Pure Clear Word,* 183; Costello, "Heartland," 228–29.
   5. Stitt, "Art of Poetry," 56.
   6. Williamson, *Introspection,* 85.
   7. McElrath, "Conversation," 135, 139; Smith, "An Interview," 31.
   8. Surely Smith errs in "Stammering Movement," 188, when he says Agnes was "the woman he did not so much love as 'he fell in with.' " Wright uses the same words to describe his love for Anne, and the phrase "heroes of love," while it admits of a crude comic reading, also serves as antithesis to the concession that Sherman never succeeded: "And he never did anything / But he fell in with Agnes."
   9. See Laurence Lieberman, Review of *Two Citizens, Yale Review* (1974), reprinted in *Unassigned Frequencies: American Poetry in Review, 1964–1977* (Urbana: University of Illinois Press, 1977), 185.
   10. Williamson, in *Introspection,* 84, offers a useful gloss on these enigmatic lines: "Names, in short, are relationships, not fixed labels; so that language and the reality it refers to come into being together, with the relation."
   11. Smith, in "Stammering Movement," 193, may overstate the mythic implication by calling this a "wonderful synthesis of an emerging butterfly and Christ's resurrection," but he comes to the provocative conclusion that the love of the earth creates the "possibility of a moral life where some things are not relative, but simply are." Similarly, Lieberman, in *Frequencies,* confuses Mary Magdelene with the mother of God, but comes to the conclusion that she is "sublimely guiltless and undespairing. Self and soul are balanced in her, the human and goddess comfortably wedded in the poet's vision of her icon" (189).

Chapter Six

1. *American Poets in 1976;* the earliest, dated 28 August 1973, appears, revised, as "Under the Canals" in *Moments of the Italian Summer,* then revised again as part 1 of "Two Moments in Venice" in *To a Blossoming Pear Tree;* Michael Benedikt, ed., *The Prose Poem* (New York: Dell, 1976); Stephen Berg and Robert Mezey, eds., *The New Naked Poetry* (Indianapolis: Bobbs-Merrill, 1976).

2. *Moments of the Italian Summer* (Washington: Dryad Press, 1977), 14.

3. Afterword to *Far from the Madding Crowd* by Thomas Hardy (New York: New American Library, 1960), 377, reprinted in *Prose,* 23–31.

4. "Two Responses to 'The Working Line,' " *Field* 8 (Spring 1973):61–65; Smith, "An Interview," 38–39.

5. Yenser, "Open Secrets," 142.

6. *To a Blossoming Pear Tree* (New York: Farrar, Straus & Giroux, 1977), 55. References in the text identify this collection as *BPT.*

7. Smith, "An Interview," 39.

8. Yenser, "Open Secrets," 150.

9. Ibid., 152.

10. "On the Occasion of a Poem: Bill Knott," 446–49.

11. McElrath, "Conversation," 139.

Selected Bibliography

PRIMARY SOURCES

1. Collection of Poems
Collected Poems. Middletown, Conn.: Wesleyan University Press, 1971.

2. Individual Volumes of Poems and Prose Poems
The Branch Will Not Break. Middletown: Wesleyan University Press, 1963.
The Green Wall. New Haven: Yale University Press, 1957.
Moments of the Italian Summer. Washington: Dryad Press, 1976.
Saint Judas. Middletown: Wesleyan University Press, 1959.
Shall We Gather at the River. Middletown: Wesleyan University Press, 1968.
The Summers of James and Annie Wright. New York: Sheep Meadow Press, 1981.
This Journey. New York: Random House, 1982.
To a Blossoming Pear Tree. New York: Farrar, Straus & Giroux, 1977.
Two Citizens. New York: Farrar, Straus & Giroux, 1973.

3. Translations (books only)
Poems. By Hermann Hesse. New York: Farrar, Straus & Giroux, 1970.
The Rider on the White Horse and Selected Stories. By Theodor Storm. New York: New American Library, 1964.
Twenty Poems of Pablo Neruda. With Robert Bly. Madison, Minn.: Sixties Press, 1967.
Twenty Poems of Georg Trakl. With Robert Bly. Madison: Sixties Press, 1961.
Twenty Poems of Cesar Vallejo. With Robert Bly and John Knoepfle. Madison: Sixties Press, 1963.
Wandering. By Hermann Hesse. With Franz Wright. New York: Farrar, Straus & Giroux, 1972.

4. Prose Collection
Collected Prose. Edited by Anne Wright. Ann Arbor: University of Michigan Press, 1983.

5. Uncollected Essays and Monographs (highly selective)
"The Comic Imagination of the Young Dickens." Ph.D. diss., University of Washington, 1959.

"Letters from Europe, Two Notes from Venice, Remarks on Two Poems, and Other Occasional Prose." In *American Poets in 1976*. Edited by William Heyen. Indianapolis: Bobbs-Merrill, 1976.

"The Music of Poetry." *American Poetry Review* 15 (March/April 1986):43–47.

"The Quest for the Child Within." Introduction to *Breathing of First Things*. By Hy Sobiloff. New York: Dial Press, 1963.

"Some Recent Poetry." *Sewanee Review* 66 (1958):657–68.

6. Interviews

Andre, Michael. "An Interview with James Wright." *Unmuzzled Ox* 1 (1972):3–18. Reprinted in *Collected Prose*.

Henricksen, Bruce. "Poetry Must Think." *New Orleans Review* 6 (1978). Reprinted in *Collected Prose*.

McElrath, Joseph R. "Something to Be Said for the Light: A Conversation with James Wright." *Southern Humanities Review* 6 (Spring 1972):134–53. Reprinted in *Collected Prose*.

Smith, Dave. "James Wright: The Pure Clear Word, an Interview." *American Poetry Review* 9 (1980):19–30. Reprinted in *The Pure Clear Word: Essays on the Poetry of James Wright*. Edited by Dave Smith. Urbana: University of Illinois Press, 1982; and in *Collected Prose*.

Stitt, Peter. "The Art of Poetry XIX: James Wright." *Paris Review* 62 (1975):35–61.

SECONDARY SOURCES

1. Bibliography

McMaster, Belle M. "James Arlington Wright: A Checklist." *Bulletin of Bibliography* 31 (1974):71–82, 88. Thorough.

2. Books and Special Issues

Ironwood 10 (1977). Special James Wright Issue. Biographical and critical essays, appreciations, original poems by Wright, tribute poems by others including Heyen, Hugo, Unterecker, Warren. Several photographs. Mentioned in the next section as *Ironwood*.

Saunders, William. *James Wright: An Introduction*. Columbus: State Library of Ohio, 1979. Brief, useful introduction.

Smith, Dave, ed. *The Pure Clear Word: Essays on the Poetry of James Wright*. Urbana: University of Illinois Press, 1982. An uneven collection of essays and one important interview. Mentioned in the next section as *Pure Clear Word*.

Stitt, Peter. *The World's Hieroglyphic Beauty: Five American Poets.* Athens: University of Georgia Press, 1985. Contains an expanded version of "The Quest Motif in *The Branch Will Not Break*" and the interview "The Art of Poetry XIX."

3. Articles and Chapters in Books (highly selective)

Auden, W. H. Foreword to *The Green Wall.* Seminal discussion of Wright's identification with outcasts.

Bly, Carol. "James Wright's Visits to Odin House, Robert Bly's Farm, Near Madison, Minnesota." *Ironwood,* 33–36. Anecdotal, personal account of the Minnesota years.

Bly, Robert. "A Note on James Wright." *Ironwood,* 64–65. Account of Wright's meeting with Bly.

Breslin, James E. B. "James Wright." In *From Modern to Contemporary: American Poetry, 1945–1965.* Chicago: University of Chicago Press, 1984. Excellent study of the schools of American poetry since World War II, in which this essay represents the "deep image" school.

Breslin, Paul. "How to Read the New Contemporary Poem." *American Scholar* 47 (1977–78):357–70. Treats Wright as exemplary of the new poetry written in America since 1960.

Butscher, Edward. "The Rise and Fall of James Wright." *Georgia Review* 28 (1974):257–68. Repr. in *Pure Clear Word.* Claims that Wright failed to live up to the promise of his talent.

Costello, Bonnie. "James Wright: Returning to the Heartland." *New Boston Review* 5 (1980):12–14. Expanded in *Pure Clear Word.* Thoughtful study of Wright's ambivalent attitudes toward his birthplace.

Crunk [Robert Bly]. "The Work of James Wright." *Sixties* 8 (1966):52–78. Repr. with an additional note in *Pure Clear Word.* Early critical account of the importance of Wright's work.

DeFrees, Madeline. "That Vacant Paradise: James Wright's Potter's Field." *Ironwood,* 13–20. A perceptive study of compassion in the early poems.

———. "James Wright's Early Poems: A Study in 'Convulsive Form.' " *Modern Poetry Studies* 2 (1972):247–51. Attempts to define the formal tensions of the early poems.

Ditsky, John. "James Wright Collected: Alterations on the Monument." *Modern Poetry Studies* 2 (1972):251–59. Excellent review-essay on *Collected Poems,* surveying Wright's achievement through 1971.

Dougherty, David. "The Executed Murderer's Grave and the New Northwest." *Old Northwest* 2 (1976):45–54. Discussion of the regional myth.

———. "The Skeptical Poetic of James Wright." *Contemporary Poetry* 11 (1977):4–10. Distrust of the motives for poetry.

Friedman, Norman. "The Wesleyan Poets III: The Experimental Poets." *Chicago Review* 19 (1967):52–73. Discusses Wright as one of the more successful experimental poets of the decade.

Harmon, William. "James Wright, the Good Poet." *Sewanee Review* 90 (1982):612–13. Biographical appreciation.

Hass, Robert. "James Wright." *Ironwood,* 74–96. Repr. in *Pure Clear Word.* Influential essay treating the themes and the communicative process of Wright's poems through 1976.

Jannsens, G. A. M. "The Present State of American Poetry: Robert Bly and James Wright." *English Studies* 5 (1970):112–37. The rationality of some deep image poets.

Lacey, Paul A. "The Scarred Truth of Wretchedness." In *The Inner War: Forms and Themes in Recent American Poetry.* Philadelphia: Fortress Press, 1972. Wright's compassion and importance as a postmodern poet.

Lieberman, Laurence. "James Wright: Words of Grass." In *Unassigned Frequencies: American Poetry In Review.* Urbana: University of Illinois Press, 1977. Perceptive reviews of *Shall We Gather* and *Two Citizens.*

Matthews, William. "The Continuity of James Wright's Poems." *Ohio Review* 18 (Spring-Summer 1977):44–57. Repr. in *Pure Clear Word.* General discussion of the evolution of the poetry.

Mills, Ralph J., Jr. "James Wright's Poetry: Introductory Notes." *Chicago Review* 17 (1964):128–43. Excellent study of the poems through 1963.

Molesworth, Charles. "James Wright and the Dissolving Self." *Salmagundi* 22–23 (1973):222–33. Repr. in *Contemporary Poetry in America.* Edited by Robert Boyers. New York: Schocken Books, 1974. Identity and Wright's persona.

Moran, Ronald, and George Lensing. "The Emotive Imagination: A New Departure in American Poetry." *Southern Review* 3 (1967):51–67. Nondiscursive and images in Wright and others.

Nathan, Leonard. "The Traditional James Wright." *Ironwood,* 131–37. Expanded to "The Tradition of Sadness and the American Metaphysic: An Interpretation of James Wright's Poetry" in *Pure Clear Word.* Associates Wright with the graveyard tradition in English poetry.

Saunders, William S. "Indignation Born of Love: James Wright's Ohio Poems." *Old Northwest* 4 (1978):353–69. Discussion of the regional myth.

Seay, James. "A World Immeasurably Alive and Good: A Look at James Wright's *Collected Poems.*" *Georgia Review* 27 (1973):71–81. Repr. in *Pure Clear Word.* Important review-essay on *Collected Poems.*

Serchuk, Peter. "On the Poet, James Wright." *Modern Poetry Studies* 10 (1981):85–90. Impressionistic, biographical tribute.

Smith, Dave. "That Halting, Stammering Movement." *Ironwood,* 111–30. Repr. in *Pure Clear Word.* Attempts to define the poetics of "New Poems" and *Two Citizens.*

Stitt, Peter. "James Wright: The Quest Motif in *The Branch Will Not Break.*" In *Pure Clear Word.* Excellent analysis of the unity of the collection.

————. "James Wright—Poetry of the Present." *Ironwood*, 140–153. Poetic
and thematic evolution beyond *The Branch.*

Taylor, Henry. "In the Mode of Robinson and Frost: James Wright's Early
Poetry." In *Pure Clear Word*. Good discussion of the first two volumes.

Williamson, Alan. "Language Against Itself: The Middle Generation of
Contemporary Poets." In *Introspection and Contemporary Poetry*. Cambridge: Harvard University Press, 1984. Provocative study of Wright
as one of the poets who tries to force language to transcend itself.

Wright, Annie. "A Horse Grazes in My Long Shadow: A Short Biography
of James Wright." *Envoy,* Spring-Summer 1981, 1–6. Brief, useful
overview of the poet's life.

————. "Fragments from a Journey." *Kenyon Review* 7 (Summer 1985):35–
43. Anecdotes from the Wright's last trip to Italy.

Yenser, Stephen. "Open Secrets." *Parnassus* 6 (1978):125–42. Repr. in
Pure Clear Word. Outstanding discussion of Wright's second revolution
in poetics.

Zweig, Paul. "Making and Unmaking." *Partisan Review* 40 (1973):269–73.
Good general criticism.

Index

Agnes (Aunt), 100–102, 148n8
Auden, W. H., 7, 17, 21–22 (quoted), 42, 79, 141
Austria, 6, 9, 52

Bedford, Ed, 2–3
Blake, William, 13, 19, 30, 99
Bly, Carol, 8
Bly, Robert, 1, 8, 13–16, 49, 52, 59 (quoted), 147n7
Braxton, Garnie, 85
Breslin, James E. B., 18, 49, 51, 146n3
Buchanan, Emerson (uncle), 93–94, 101

Catullus, 5, 17, 71, 92, 122–23, 125
Cecilia, Saint, 109–11
Chessman, Caryl, 12, 44
City, the, 30, 22, 79–82
Costello, Bonnie, 75, 95, 147n5

Daley, Richard, 134–35
"Dalliance of Eagles, The" (Whitman), 108–9
Dante, 98, 140
Daphne, 89, 99
deep image, 1, 14–16, 51–52, 53, 54, 81, 141
DeFrees, Madeline, 18, 31 (quoted), 50
Depression, Great (1930s), 4–6, 62, 65, 103, 120
"De Profundis" (Trakl), 52–54
Dickens, Charles, 6, 7, 9, 17, 80
Dickey, James, 8, 45–46, 49
"Directive" (Frost), 134
Ditsky, John, 43
Doty, George, 12, 44–47, 54, 113
Doty, Ernie, 77

Eisenhower, Dwight David, 59–60
Eliot, T. S., 1, 6, 20, 21, 98, 106, 140
elegy, 11–12, 29, 34, 40, 90, 102, 122, 133–36

Enscoe, Gerald, 32–33
Esterley, Elizabeth (teacher), 5, 8
Eucharist, 59, 110–12

Far From the Madding Crowd (Hardy), 115
"Fern Hill" (Thomas), 127–28
Flower Herding on Mount Monadnock (Kinnell), 49
"Four Quartets" (Eliot), 140
Franco, Francisco, 59–60
Freud, Sigmund, 46, 54
Frost, Robert, 12, 17, 18, 21, 27, 35, 51, 64, 94, 134
Frye, Northrop, 15

Hanna, Mark, 65, 99
Harding, Warren G., 12, 60–62, 76, 113, 125
Hardy, Thomas, 9, 11, 12, 17, 18, 34, 64, 94, 97, 115
Hass, Robert, 147n8
Heilman, Robert, 7, 8
Hemingway, Ernest, 36, 94–95, 102
Hesse, Hermann, 56, 114–15
Hoover, J. Edgar, 64, 73–74
Hoover, Herbert, 61
Horace, 5, 6, 16, 17, 33, 52, 95–96, 111, 122–23
Hugo, Richard, 1, 36
Hunter College, 9

Indians, American, 12, 62, 79, 91–92, 131–32
Ironwood (special James Wright Issue), 133

Jannsens, G. A. M., 51
Jeffers, Robinson, 20, 42, 89, 132
Jenny (muse), 11, 30, 75–78, 80, 85, 95, 99, 102, 104, 105, 106, 109, 110, 113

Jesus Christ, 27, 42, 47, 53, 79, 98–99, 103–4, 110–11, 120, 135, 136–37, 138–39, 148n11
Job, Book of, 78
Joyce, James, 97, 104
Judas Iscariot, 42–44, 99
Jung, C. G., 15, 24

Kardules, Liberty. *See* Wright, Liberty
Kelly, Robert, 14–15
Kenyon College, 6, 11, 20
King Lear (Shakespeare), 31, 131–32
Kinnell, Galway, 9, 10, 14, 20, 49, 133
Knight, Etheridge, 127–28

Lacey, Paul, 43
Lensing, George, 52, 147n3
Leonard, Jimmy, 41
Leonard, Minnegan, 41, 61, 113
Lieberman, Laurence, 148n11
"Lines Composed a Few Miles Above Tintern Abbey" (Wordsworth), 35, 64
Little Crow (Sioux chief), 12, 91–92
Livingston, Ray, 71, 83
"Love Song of J. Alfred Prufrock, The" (Eliot), 98, 106
Lowell, Robert, 11, 19, 49, 54–55, 122
"Lycidas" (Milton), 135
Lyons, Willy (uncle), 11, 87–88, 134, 135

Macalester College, 8, 83
Machado, Antonio, 59
Magdalene, Mary, 109–12, 148n11
Maguire, 24
Martins Ferry (Ohio), 4–5, 6, 10, 46, 57, 80, 86, 97, 102–4, 119, 124, 134
Matthews, William, 18, 53
Merwin, W. S., 12, 20
Michelangelo, 109
Midsummer Night's Dream, A (Shakespeare), 130
Millay, Edna St. Vincent, 88–90
Mills, Ralph J., Jr., 43
Minneapolis (Minnesota), 7, 57, 78–82, 87, 91, 130–33

Minnesota, University of, 7–8, 87
Mississippi River, 73
modernism, 19–21, 141
Molesworth, Charles, 15 (quoted)
monologue, dramatic, 26, 27, 30, 34, 42, 92
Moran, Ronald, 51, 147

Nathan, Leonard, 75
Neal, Ralph, 120–21
Neruda, Pablo, 10, 14, 15, 17
Nevada, 62–63, 84

Ohio River, 4–6, 58, 72–73, 76, 78, 96–97, 103, 117, 124–25, 126, 135–36
Olson, Charles, 1, 19
open forms, 13, 19, 50–52, 58, 69, 93, 121, 142

Plath, Sylvia, 19, 54
poetry, confessional, 15, 19–20, 54–55, 70–71, 141
poetry, postmodern, 1, 3, 69, 124
poets, academic, 19–21, 22, 27, 30, 35, 49, 141
Pound, Ezra, 1, 14, 19, 20
"prose pieces," 114–21

Ransom, John Crowe, 6, 11–12, 15, 20, 29, 35, 84
Raphael, 109–12
Richard III (Shakespeare), 70
Robinson, Edwin Arlington, 11, 12, 17, 18, 21, 42, 46, 64, 94, 97, 102, 112, 122
Roethke, Theodore, 6, 7, 12–13, 15
Romeo and Juliet (Shakespeare), 128–30
Runk, Edith Anne. *See* Wright, Anne

Sappho, 26–27, 103
Seay, James, 49
sentimentality, 3, 24
Shakespeare, William, 70, 83, 128–30, 131–32
Sheriff, Helen McNeeley (teacher), 5
Silence in the Snowy Fields (Bly), 49
Smith, Dave, 95, 148n8, 148n11
Snodgrass, W. D., 19, 20

sonnet, 24, 30, 42–43, 55, 122
Stepanchev, Stephen, 49
Sterne, Laurence, 8, 9, 76
Stevens, Wallace, 20, 32–33
Stitt, Peter, 55, 56 (quoted), 67, 148n5
Storm, Theodor, 6
surrealism, 1, 14–16, 52, 65
Swift, Jonathan, 9, 30, 61, 89

Tate, Allen, 20, 46
Taylor, Henry, 18, 19
Tempest, The (Shakespeare), 130
Thomas, Dylan, 127–28
Timberlake, Philip, 6
Trakl, Georg, 14, 17, 52–54
Tristram Shandy (Sterne), 8, 76

Updike, John, 2–3

Vallejo, Cesar, 14
Verona (Italy), 117–18, 119, 123, 124–26, 128–30
Vienna (Austria), 6, 9
Vietnam war, 14, 92, 103, 142
Virgil, 54, 94, 122–23

Warren, Robert Penn, 1–2, 3
Washington, University of, 6, 7, 12–13
Wheeling (West Virginia), 4, 57, 72, 78, 119
Whitman, Walt, 17, 19, 32–34, 35, 51, 64, 81–82, 108–9, 128, 137
Wilbur, Richard, 12, 20, 22, 49
Williams, William Carlos, 19, 20, 67, 68, 73, 109, 127
Williamson, Alan, 51–52, 54, 94–95, 147n5, 148n10
Wordsworth, William, 35, 51, 64, 137
Wright, Anne, 9–10, 85, 96–97, 101, 104–9, 114, 115, 133, 148n8
Wright, Dudley (father), 4–5, 9, 46, 62, 86–87, 95–97, 103, 119–20
Wright, Franz Paul (son), 6, 90, 96, 114–15
Wright, Jack (brother), 85, 87
Wright, James Arlington: academic affiliations, 7–9, 83, 87; army service, 5; artistic legacy, 141–43; childhood and early education, 4–6, 120–21;

college and graduate study, 6–7, 11, 12; death, 10, 133; European travel, 6, 9–10, 104–5; influenced by Bly, 13–17; influenced by Ransom, 10–12; influenced by Roethke, 12–13; influenced by Trakl, 14, 17, 52–54; marriages, 6–10, 87, 104–5

WORKS: POEMS
"Accusation, The," 38–39
"Afternoon and Evening at Ohrid," 107–8
"All the Beautiful Are Blameless," 37, 38
"American Twilights, 1957," 42, 44
"American Wedding," 67
"Angel, The," 27
"Arrangements with Earth for Three Dead Friends," 12, 29–30
"Arriving in the Country Again," 67
"Ars Poetica: Some Recent Criticism," 100–102, 122–23
"Art of the Fugue, The: A Prayer," 105
"As I Step Over a Puddle at the End of Winter, I Think of an Ancient Chinese Governor," 49, 57, 63
"At the Executed Murderer's Grave," 14, 31, 39, 42, 45–48, 54, 56, 86
"At the Grave," 6
"At the Slackening of the Tide," 37–38
"Autumn Begins In Martins Ferry, Ohio," 57–58, 79–80
"Before a Cashier's Window in a Department Store," 83–84
"Beginning," 68
"Best Days, The," 123, 124
"Between Wars," 122
"Blessing, A," 68, 90, 143
"Bologna: A Poem About Gold," 109–12, 113, 143
Branch Will Not Break, The, 8, 18, 19, 40, 48, 49–68, 69, 84, 93, 96, 113, 116, 117, 121, 123, 124, 128
"Centenary Ode, A: Inscribed to Little Crow, Leader of the Sioux Re-

bellion, 1862," 91–92
"Chilblain," 87, 134
Collected Poems, 9, 10, 49, 53, 62, 69, 90, 91, 93
"Come Forth," 27
"Complaint," 34–35
"Confession to J. Edgar Hoover," 16, 73–74, 136

"Dark Moor Bird, A," 137
"Depressed By a Book of Bad Poetry, I Walk Toward an Unused Pasture and Invite the Insects to Join Me," 49–50, 68
"De Profundis" (translation), 52–53

"Echo for the Promise of Georg Trakl's Life," 52
"Eclogue at Nash's Grove," 90, 123
"Eisenhower's Visit to Franco, 1959," 58–60
"Emerson Buchanan," 93–94, 97, 104
"Erinna to Sappho," 27
"Evening," 12

"Fear is What Quickens Me," 66–67
"Finch Sitting Out a Windstorm, A," 137–38
"First Days, The," 123, 124
"Fishing Song, A," 90
"Fit Against the Country, A," 27
"Flower Passage, A *(in memory of Joe Shank, the diver),*" 135–36

"Gambling in Stateline, Nevada," 84
"Gesture by a Lady with an Assumed Name, A," 22–24, 110
"Goodbye to the Poetry of Calcium," 50–52
Green Wall, The, 7, 12, 19, 21–30, 42, 44, 79

"Having Lost My Sons, I Confront the Wreckage of the Moon: Christmas, 1960," 7, 60, 62, 115
"Hook," 124, 130–32
"Horse, The," 27
"Humming a Tune for an Old Lady in West Virginia," 72, 106

"I Am a Sioux Brave, He Said in Minneapolis," 131
"I Wish I May Never Hear of the United States Again," 100
"Idea of the Good, The," 75, 99, 103–4
"In Defense of Late Summer," 121–22
"In Memory of a Spanish Poet," 58–59
"In Memory of Mayor Richard Daley," 134–35
"In Memory of the Horse David, Who Ate One of My Poems," 8
"In Response to a Rumor that the Oldest Whorehouse in Wheeling, West Virginia, Has Been Condemned," 72, 78
"In Shame and Humiliation," 5
"In the Cold House," 67
"In the Face of Hatred," 66
"In Terror of Hospital Bills," 70, 83
"Inscription for the Tank," 70–71, 83

"Jerome in Solitude," 136–37
"Jewel, The," 66, 105–6, 125
"Journey, The," 139–40

"Katy Did," 71–72

"Lament: Fishing with Richard Hugo," 1, 146n8
"Lament for My Brother on a Hayrake," 27
"Last Drunk, The," 115
"Last Pieta in Florence, The," 109
"Late November in a Field," 71
"Lighting a Candle for W. H. Auden," 141
"Lying in a Hammock at William Duffy's Farm in Pine Island, Minnesota," 54–56

"Mad Song for William S. Carpenter, A," 72, 92, 136
"Many of Our Waters: Variations on a Poem by a Black Child," 3, 69, 71–73, 78–82, 85, 93, 114
"March," 67
"Mary Bly," 64
"Message Hidden in an Empty Wine

Bottle that I Threw Into a Gully of Maple Trees One Night at an Indecent Hour," 67
"Miners," 16, 63
"Minneapolis Poem, The," 7, 69, 73, 78–82, 126, 131
Moments of the Italian Summer, 114, 115–16, 119
"Morality of Poetry, The," 31–34, 51
"Morning Hymn to a Dark Girl," 30
"Mutterings Over the Crib of a Deaf Child," 24, 25–26

"Names Scarred Over the Entrance to Chartres," 104
"New Poems," 62, 68, 69–92, 93, 94, 95, 113, 116, 142
"Northern Pike," 90–91
"Note Left in Jimmy Leonard's Shack, A," 41, 50, 60
"Notes of a Pastoralist," 136

"October Ghosts," 75, 95, 97, 102, 105
"Offense, The," 83, 131
"Offering for Mr. Bluehart, An," 39–41
"Ohio Valley Swains," 84, 97–99, 101, 102, 120, 138
"Old Man Drunk," 35–36
"Old WPA Swimming Pool in Martins Ferry, Ohio, The," 97, 103–4, 120
"On a Hostess Saying Good Night," 6
"On a Phrase From Southern Ohio," 127–28
"On Minding One's Own Business," 35–37
"One Last Look at the Adige: Verona in the Rain," 122, 124–26

"Paul" *(Saint Judas),* 34
"Paul" *(Two Citizens),* 97, 102–3, 120
"Poem About George Doty in the Death House, A," 44–45
"Poems to a Brown Cricket," 69, 85–86

"Prayer to Escape the Market Place, A," 68
"Prayer to the Good Poet," 33, 95–96, 111
"Rain," 67
"Reading a 1979 Inscription on Belli's Monument," 24, 122
"Red Jacket's Grave," 91
"Redwings," 126–27
"RIP," 86

"Saint Jerome," 136–37
"Saint Judas," 24, 34, 42–44, 99, 122, 136
Saint Judas, 7, 17, 18–19, 30–47, 48, 49, 50, 51, 56, 93, 94, 113, 121
"Sappho," 26–27
"Secret Gratitude, A," 69, 88–90, 99
Shall We Gather at the River, 8, 49, 68, 69–88, 93, 94, 95, 96, 104, 105, 123, 134, 142
"She Hid in Trees from the Nurses," 24–25
"Small Blue Heron, The," 88
"Small Frogs Killed on the Highway," 123
"Snowstorm in the Midwest," 64
"So She Said," 86
"Son of Judas," 95, 99, 107
"Speak," 75, 76–78, 102
"Stages on a Journey Westward," 60, 62–63, 91, 134
Summers of James and Annie Wright, The, 9, 10, 133

This Journey, 10, 90, 114, 116, 119, 122–23, 133–40
"Three Sentences for a Dead Swan," 72, 88
"To a Blossoming Pear Tree," 124, 130–31, 132–33
To a Blossoming Pear Tree, 9, 112, 113–33, 141
"To a Dead Drunk," 71, 72
"To a Defeated Savior," 28–29
"To a Friendly Dun," 83
"To a Fugitive," 24–25, 26

"To Flood Stage Again," 73
"To the Cicada," 138–39
"To the Muse," 75–76, 102
"To You Out There (Mars? Jupiter?)",
    104
"Today I Was So Happy, So I Made
    this Poem," 64
"Twilights," 67
Two Citizens, 68, 75, 86, 87, 92,
    93–112, 113, 114, 115, 116, 121,
    122, 124, 142, 143
"Two Hangovers," 54–66, 67, 137
"Two Horses Playing in the Or-
    chard," 50
"Two Poems About President Har-
    ding," 60–62, 76, 125
"Two Postures Beside a Fire," 86–87

"Undermining of the Defense Econ-
    omy, The," 58

"Villanelle for the New Soldiers," 7
"Voices Between Waking and Sleep-
    ing in the Mountains," 105–7

Wandering (Hesse), 56, 114–15
"Way to Make a Living, A," 86
"What the Earth Asked Me," 34
"Willy Lyons," 87
"With the Shell of a Hermit Crab,"
    121, 122
"Written on a Big Cheap Postcard
    From Verona," 128–30, 131
"You and I Saw Hawks Exchanging
    the Prey," 108–9
"Youth," 86

WORKS: "PROSE PIECES"
"Against Surrealism," 16
"Flying Eagles of Troop 62, The,"
    120–21
"Fruits of the Season, The," 116
"Honey," 5
"Lament For the Shadows in the
    Ditches, A," 117
"Secret of Light, The," 117–19
"Wheeling Gospel Tabernacle, The,"
    119–20, 138

WORKS: ESSAYS
"Delicacy of Walt Whitnam, The,"
    34, 146n7
"Note on Georg Trakl, A," 52–53
"On the Occasion of a Poem: Bill
    Knott," 134, 149n9
"Stiff Smile of Mr. Warren, The,"
    1–2, 145n1

Wright, Jessie (mother), 4, 9, 86, 87,
    119–20
Wright, Liberty (wife), 6, 7–8
Wright, Marshall (son), 7, 90
Wright, Theodore (brother), 12

Yeats, William, 13, 35
Yenser, Stephen, 116, 127, 147n5,
    148n3

Zweig, Paul, 49, 73